# POSITIVE BEHAVIOUR SUPPORT STRATEGIES FOR STUDENTS WITH ANXIOUS BEHAVIOUR

A step by step guide to assessing, preventing and managing emotional and behavioural difficulties

## DOLLY BHARGAVA

**Masters in Special Education**

Copyright ©2020, Behaviour Help Pty Ltd.

The contents of this book (text and graphics) are protected by international copyright law. No part of this publication may be reproduced, stored in a retrieval system, transmitted, broadcast or communicated in any form or by any means, optical, digital, electronic, mechanical, photocopying, recording or otherwise, without the written permission of Dolly Bhargava. To obtain permission, email: admin@behaviourhelp.com

Target behaviour data collection forms can be reproduced with citation: Bhargava, D. (2020). Positive Behaviour Support Strategies for Students with Anxious Behaviour: A Step by Step Guide to Assessing, Preventing and Managing Emotional and Behavioural Difficulties (2nd Edition). Melbourne VIC: Behaviour Help Pty Ltd.

**Disclaimer:** The information set out in this booklet is of a general nature only and not exhaustive on the subject matter. The information may or may not be relevant in particular to your student's circumstance. This book should not be used as a diagnostic tool. Persons implementing any recommendations contained in this publication must exercise their own independent skill or judge mentor seek appropriate professional advice relevant to their own circumstances when so doing.

Note: In this book we have used the term 'student' to refer to children, adolescents and adults with Anxiety Disorder or who exhibit anxious behaviour.

# CONTENTS

- CONTENTS ............................................................................................. iii
- INTRODUCTION ....................................................................................... i
- DEFINING ANXIOUS BEHAVIOUR ............................................................ 1
- ASSESS STAGE CHECKLIST RESOURCES: TASKS ................................. 9
- POSITIVE BEHAVIOUR SUPPORT STRATEGIES: MANAGE STAGE ........ 35
- POSITIVE BEHAVIOUR SUPPORT STRATEGIES: PREVENT STAGE ....... 63
- CONCLUDING REMARK ......................................................................... 75
- REFERENCES ........................................................................................ 77
- OTHER TITLES BY DOLLY BHARGAVA ................................................. 79

# INTRODUCTION

All students experience difficulties with managing their emotions and behaviours at one time or another. With understanding, support and encouragement, most students learn the skills they need to manage their own emotions and behaviours. However, students who exhibit anxious behaviours or have a diagnosis of an Anxiety Disorder repeatedly engage in emotional and behavioural responses that can cause serious harm to others and/ or themselves. Despite best efforts and intentions, the student has difficulties learning how to manage their emotions and behaviours, and the situation doesn't appear to improve.

As a parent, teacher, support staff member or professional, directly facing the student's challenging emotional and behavioural responses daily can leave you feeling stressed, exhausted and disheartened. If any of this sounds familiar, then you have come to the right place.

This book will provide you with a roadmap developed from the evidenced based approach of Positive Behaviour Support (PBS) to help you guide the student learn positive ways of behaving and managing their emotions.

Through your persistence, patience and perseverance you can make a difference in your student's life. The road to behaviour change begins with the first step. I would like to take this opportunity to commend you for taking the first step in this journey to build a better future for your student.

Best wishes on the journey.

*Dolly Bhargava*

# DEFINING ANXIOUS BEHAVIOUR

All of us experience some degree of anxiety (i.e. fear and worry) from time to time. When faced with a stressful situation (e.g. first day of school, giving a job interview or preparing for an exam) it is expected, normal and useful that we experience a little bit of anxiety. Anxiety experienced within the normal range is short lived and we return to a calm state when the stressful situation is over. However, for some students their worries and fears last for long periods of time. This can affect the student's ability to learn, participate and get along with others.

This book contains information for students who exhibit anxious behaviours as well as those students who have a diagnosis of an Anxiety Disorder.

The Diagnostic and Statistical Manual of Mental Disorders 5th edition (DSM-5) [American Psychiatric Publishing (APA), 2013], is a handbook that is used by professionals around the world to diagnose mental disorders. Below are some of the common types of Anxiety Disorders with

- ☐ Separation anxiety disorder – Excessive anxiety about anticipated or actual separation from caregiver/s.

- ☐ Selective mutism - Excessive anxiety resulting in an inability to speak in a social situation/s, despite being able to speak in others.

- ☐ Specific phobia – Excessive, irrational fear or anxiety about or avoidance of facing a specific object, or situation.

- ☐ Social anxiety disorder – Excessive anxiety about or avoidance of social or performance situations that involve the possibility of negative judgements and evaluation by others which may result in embarrassment, rejection or cause offence to others.

- ☐ Panic disorder – Characterised by sudden and repeated episodes of intense fear and panic attacks.

- Generalised anxiety disorder – Excessive and persistent worry about different aspects of life.

## Causes

There is no single cause of anxious behaviours. Instead, it is the product of the interaction between multiple risk factors. They include:

- Genetics (i.e. differences in one's genetic code and/or inherited genes that makes one susceptible for developing the disorder)

- Brain chemistry (i.e. imbalance in chemicals in the brain that regulate feelings and physical reactions)

- Personality factors (e.g. being a perfectionist, having low self-esteem, becoming easily flustered or wanting to control everything)

- Medical conditions (e.g. diabetes, thyroid problems, heart disease and respiratory disorders)

- Stressful events such as loss (e.g. death of a loved one or a pet, parents' divorce), major life change (e.g. change of school, moving to a new country) and leading a high stress lifestyle (e.g. student is doing too many extracurricular activities)

- Drug and alcohol abuse

## Associated Behavioural and Emotional Difficulties:

The student may exhibit some or all of following:

- ☐ Show excessive fear, concern or worry about particular tasks/situations/places

- ☐ Refuse to join in or avoid particular subjects/activities/places

- ☐ Appear extremely self-conscious or uncomfortable in social situations

- ☐ Socially isolate self, withdraw or appear very shy in social situations

- ☐ Often ask to go to sick bay due to physical complaints (e.g. headaches, stomach aches)

- ☐ Trouble with concentrating, appear distracted or forgetful

- ☐ Require lots of reassurance

- ☐ Get easily frustrated and is reluctant to ask for help

- ☐ Be a perfectionist or procrastinate and take longer to complete a task

- ☐ Decline in performance

- ☐ Engage in unhealthy, risky or self-destructive behaviour (e.g. drug or alcohol abuse)

- ☐ Be very sensitive to perceived or real criticism and corrective feedback

## POSITIVE BEHAVIOUR SUPPORT DEFINED

Positive Behaviour Support (PBS) is an evidenced-based implementation framework that is designed to enhance academic, social and behavioural outcomes for all students. PBS recognises that all behaviour serves a purpose.

PBS emphasises the need for an assessment to take place to understand the reason for specific behaviours before a comprehensive intervention plan is developed. Based on the assessment findings, PBS uses multiple approaches to reduce behaviours of concern by changing interactions, altering environments, teaching skills, and appreciating behaviour (Carr et al., 1994; Horner and Diemer, 1992; Sugai and Simonsen, 2012). Think about the student you support. What do you wish for the student to achieve academically? socially? behaviourally?

_____

_____

_____

## POSITIVE BEHAVIOUR SUPPORT TEAM

Dealing with the student's challenging emotional and behavioural difficulties alone can be extremely stressful, demoralising and disheartening. It is also unlikely that any one person will have all of the answers to all of the challenges.

Hence, it is useful to identify a group of people who know the student well (e.g. parents), other teaching staff (e.g. class teachers, education assistants, specialist teachers), allied health professionals (e.g. psychologist, speech pathologist, occupational therapist) and school administration staff (e.g. principal, deputy principal).

Each person on the team can bring their own unique knowledge and perspective. By working in partnership, you can jointly come up with a plan to address the student's emotional and behavioural difficulties. Also, when everyone works together in a unified manner the team can effectively support each other and ultimately help the student reach their potential.

Think of all the people that will be involved in helping the student through the PBS strategies stages. Record their name/s:

| Team member name | Role | Setting they support the student in (e.g. home, day centre, school) |
|---|---|---|
|  |  |  |
|  |  |  |
|  |  |  |
|  |  |  |
|  |  |  |
|  |  |  |
|  |  |  |

## POSITIVE BEHAVIOUR SUPPORT STAGES

The journey of transformation is a lifelong process of growth and development. Learning effective emotional management and behavioural skills is an ongoing cycle that involves continuous refining and adapting of skills according to the expectations, people and situations encountered. Therefore, it is critical that as parents, teachers, support staff and professionals we recognise that as the student faces new challenges and demands they will need our guidance.

PBS utilises a cyclical ongoing process that consists of three stages: assess-manage-prevent.

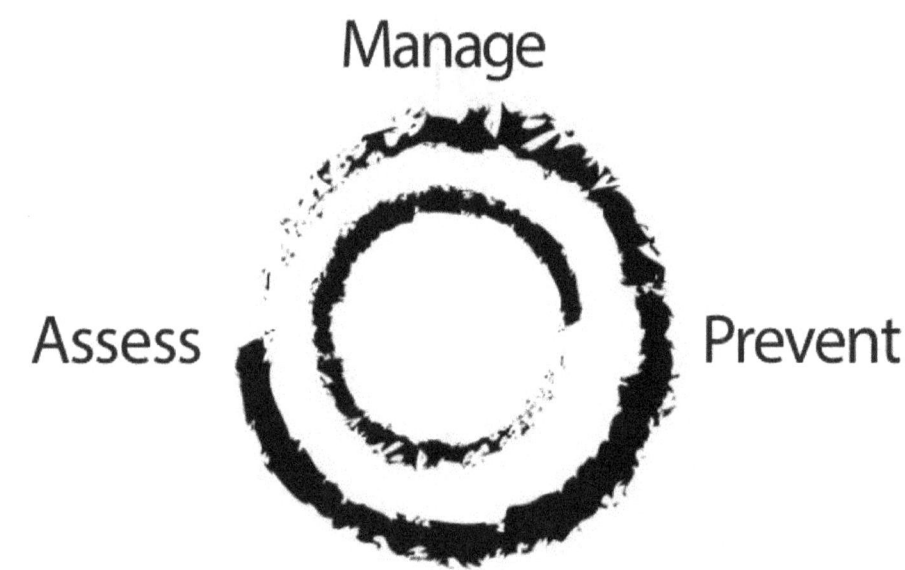

# POSITIVE BEHAVIOUR SUPPORT STRATEGIES: ASSESS STAGE

Emotional and behavioural difficulties do not occur in a vacuum, but within a context. The context involves an interaction between the student, other people and the environment. The first stage of the journey is to assess this complex relationship as shown below:

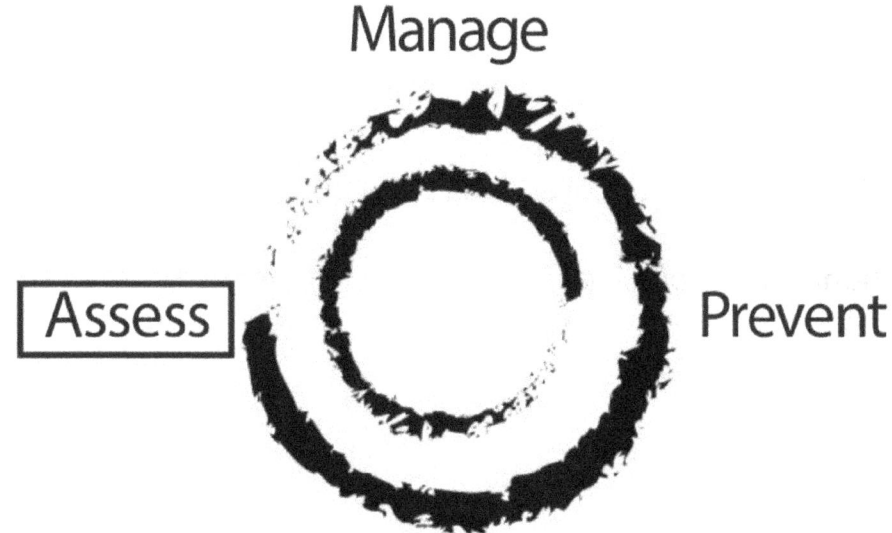

Assessment is a process of engaging in detective work in order to understand the message (function) that the student is communicating through their emotional and behavioural difficulties. In other words, the assess stage helps to identity the:

1. activity/s in which the student engages in emotional and behavioural difficulties,

2. environment/s in which the student engages in emotional and behavioural difficulties, and

3. people with whom the student engages in emotional and behavioural difficulties. Once problematic interactions have been identified, the underlying reason/s for a student's emotional and behavioural difficulties can be investigated.

Once problematic interactions have been identified, the underlying reason/s for a student's emotional and behavioural difficulties can be investigated.

**Assess Stage Checklist**

To determine why a student is engaging in the emotional and behavioural difficulties, you will need to work through each of the checklist tasks with your team.

Task 1 Student Profile

Task 2 Target Behaviour Data Collection Forms

Task 3 Functional Behaviour Analysis using Behaviour Help web-based app

# ASSESS STAGE CHECKLIST RESOURCES: TASKS

## TASK 1: STUDENT PROFILE

Identify the people, who may or may not be part of the team, who know the student well. Give them each a copy of the Student Profile and ask them to answer the questions as appropriate. The information from all of the profiles can then be collated to help create a comprehensive picture of who the student is.

Student Name: _____ Date: _____

Contributor name/s: _____

Describe the student's general health: _____

Describe the student's communication skills: _____

Describe the student's social skills: _____

Describe the student's academic skills: _____

Describe the student's problem-solving skills: _____

Describe the student's interests, likes and dislikes: _____

Describe major life events the student has experienced: _____

Think of all the emotional and behavioural difficulties the student engages in. Prioritise one behaviour that is of immediate concern to target.

1. What does it look like? _____

2. What does it sound like? _____

3. How often does it occur? _____

4. How long does it last? _____

5. Where does it occur? _____

6. With whom does it occur? _____

7. When did the student commence displaying this behaviour? _____

8. Why do you think the student engages in the behaviour? _____

9. What intervention strategies have you used in the past to attempt to change the student's behaviour?
_____

Other: _____

10. Complete the table below by writing out a typical routine in your environment. Next to each activity, indicate whether the target behaviour is likely or unlikely to occur.

*Positive Behaviour Support Strategies for Students with Anxious Behaviour*

| Time | Activity | Likelihood of the target behaviour occurring (likely or unlikely) |
|------|----------|------------------------------------------------------------------|
|      |          |                                                                  |
|      |          |                                                                  |
|      |          |                                                                  |
|      |          |                                                                  |

Other: _____

_____

## TASK 2: TARGET BEHAVIOUR DATA COLLECTION

By observing how the student interacts with various people, in different activities and in different environments, you can record the details of emotional and behavioural difficulties as they occur. Make a list of all the emotional and behavioural difficulties the student exhibits, prioritise them, and select one that is of immediate concern.

Student's name: _____

Recorder name: _____

Date: _____

Setting/Environment:

_____

Describe behaviour in specific, observable and measurable terms:

_____

Answer the following questions to identify the appropriate data collection form/s you need to complete:

1. Does the target behaviour happen so often that an accurate count is impossible?

    ☐ Yes (Go to Q. 5)
    ☐ No (Go to Q. 2)

2. Does the target behaviour have a clear beginning and end?

    ☐ Yes (Complete Frequency Recording Form and then go to Q. 3)
    ☐ No (Go to Q. 3)

3. Does the target behaviour start and stop too rapidly to record?

    ☐ Yes (Go to Q. 5)
    ☐ No (Go to Q. 4)

4. Is the length of time the student engages in the target behaviour a concern?

    ☐ Yes (Complete Duration Recording Form and then go to Q. 5)
    ☐ No (Go to Q. 5)

5. Does the target behaviour differ in intensity (e.g. mild, moderate or severe)?

    ☐ Yes (Complete Intensity Recording Form)
    ☐ No (log on to Behaviour Help web-based app)

## Behaviour Frequency Recording Form

Student's name: _____

Recorder name: _____

Procedure: To document the number of times the behaviour occurs, divide your observation time into intervals or blocks (e.g. 5 min blocks, 10 min blocks, 30 min blocks or 1-hour blocks). Complete the time interval column accordingly (e.g. if you are observing from 8:30am–10am over three consecutive days for two weeks, record the time intervals: 8:30am–9:00am; 9:00am–9:30am; 9:30am–10am and list the dates of recording). During your observation, place a tally mark in the corresponding box every time the target behaviour occurs. At the end of the time interval, count the total number of tally marks.

| Time interval | Target behaviour occurrence/s on date: | Target behaviour occurrence/s on date: | Target behaviour occurrence/s on date: | Target behaviour occurrence/s on date: |
|---|---|---|---|---|
|  | Total | Total | Total | Total |
|  | Total | Total | Total | Total |
|  | Total | Total | Total | Total |
|  | Total | Total | Total | Total |
|  | Total | Total | Total | Total |

## Identify any patterns:

Are there any times of the day when it is most likely that the student will engage in the target behaviour?

_____

_____

Are there any times of the day when it is least likely that the student will engage in the target behaviour?

_____

_____

## Behaviour Duration Recording Form

Student's name: _____

Recorder name: _____

Procedure: To document how long the student engages in the behaviour for, record the time the target behaviour started and the time it ended each time you observe it. Calculate the length of time that the behaviour lasted and write it in minutes and/or seconds.

| Date | Time target behaviour started | Time target behaviour ended | Total duration of target behaviour |
|---|---|---|---|
|  |  |  |  |
|  |  |  |  |
|  |  |  |  |
|  |  |  |  |
|  |  |  |  |
|  |  |  |  |

**Identify any patterns:**

What is the average duration of the target behaviour?

_____

_____

What is the longest duration of the target behaviour?

_____

_____

## Behaviour Intensity Recording Form

Student's name: _____ Recorder name: _____

Procedure: To document the level/degree of strength/force/volume of the behaviour, decide on a rating system to describe the intensity of the behaviour. For example, mild – moderate – severe or on a scale of 1 to 5 where 1 is least severe and 5 is most severe. Every time you observe the target behaviour, rate its severity.

| Date | Time | Behaviour Rating |
|------|------|------------------|
|      |      |                  |
|      |      |                  |
|      |      |                  |
|      |      |                  |
|      |      |                  |
|      |      |                  |
|      |      |                  |

**Identify any patterns when the intensity of the behaviour is low vs. high:**

_____

_____

## TASK 3: FUNCTIONAL BEHAVIOUR ANALYSIS (FBA)

Once the behaviour data collection forms have been completed, the next step is to work out why the student engages in emotional and behavioural difficulties. A Functional Behaviour Analysis (FBA) is a process that involves reflecting on an incident where the target behaviour occurred in an effort to identify what triggered it and the purpose (function) the target behaviour served. To complete the FBA, you will need to log on to the Behaviour Help web-based app (www.behaviourhelp.com). Once you have logged on and recorded your student's name you can systematically analyse a recent incident by carrying out an FBA. Start by selecting 'document incident'.

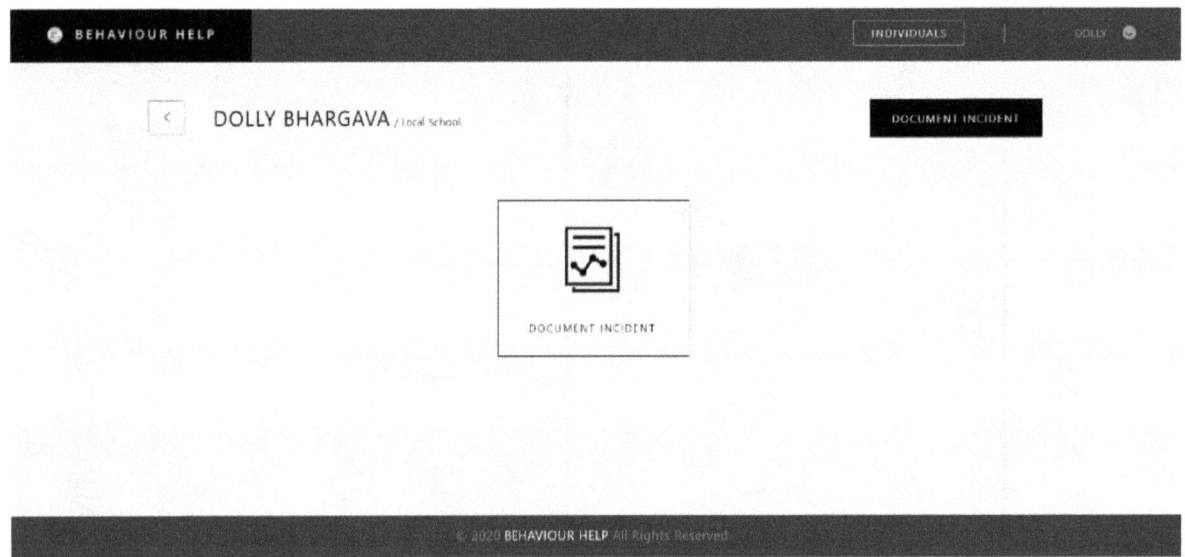

# TASK 3: FBA ↦ COMPLETE 'RECORD INCIDENT'

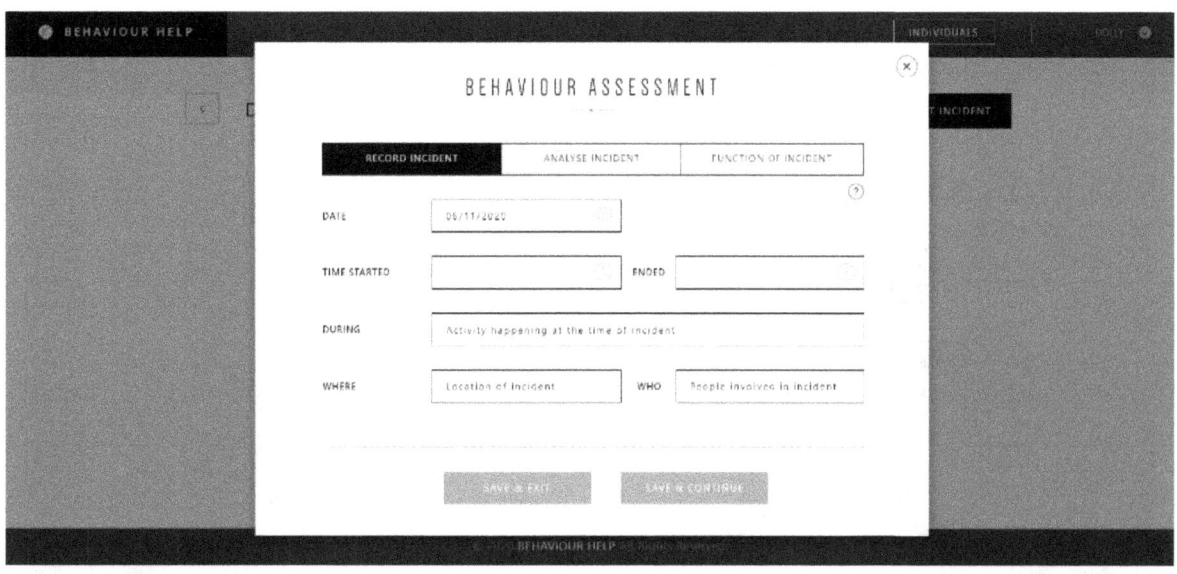

| WHAT? | Record the contextual details of the incident. |
|---|---|
| WHY? | By recording these details we can learn from them and, if possible, identify a pattern and prevent their recurrence. |
| HOW? | DATE – Record the date the incident occurred<br>TIME STARTED – Record the time the incident started<br>ENDED – Record the time the incident finished<br>DURING – Record the activity that was happening at the time of the incident<br>WHERE – Record the location of the incident<br>WHO – Record the names of people who were involved in the incident |

# TASK 3: FBA ↦ COMPLETE 'ANALYSE INCIDENT' ↦ ANTECEDENT

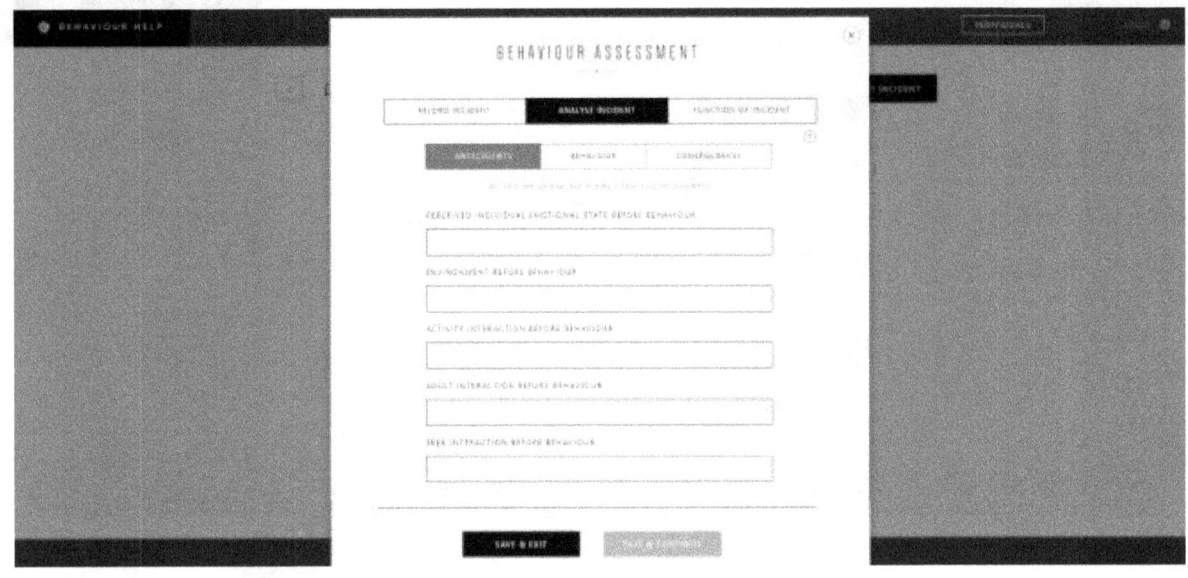

| WHAT? | Record the events (antecedents) that immediately preceded the behaviour. |
|---|---|
| WHY? | This will help you identify events that set off the student's behaviour (triggers) and events that do not set off the behaviour. This information can then be used to identify intervention strategies to prevent and manage the behaviour in the future. |
| HOW? | With the help of your team, identify which of the subheadings listed on the next page and/or in the Behaviour Help web-based app refer to what triggered the student's behaviour. For the selected subheadings, select the options that apply and/or edit the text as appropriate. If recorded on paper, enter the information in the web-based app. |

# TASK 3: ANTECEDENT

| | |
|---|---|
| Perceived student emotional state before behaviour | ☐ Seemed unsafe ☐ Seemed scared<br>☐ Seemed bored ☐ Seemed upset<br>☐ Seemed overexcited ☐ Seemed angry<br>☐ Seemed tired ☐ Seemed thirsty<br>☐ Seemed unwell ☐ Seemed tense<br>☐ Seemed hungry ☐ Seemed in pain<br>☐ Seemed worried ☐ Seemed uncomfortable |
| Environmental context before behaviour | ☐ Transition between environments ☐ Too hot<br>☐ Unfamiliar environment ☐ Too cold<br>☐ Non-preferred environment |
| | Olfactory (smell) aspect<br>☐ Environment had a strong odour<br>☐ Environment had a non-preferred odour<br>☐ Environment had a preferred odour |
| | Proprioceptive (body awareness) aspect<br>☐ Had insufficient personal space |
| | Auditory aspect<br>☐ Environment was too noisy<br>☐ Environment was too quiet |
| | Visual aspect<br>☐ Environment had bright lights ☐ Environment was visually cluttered<br>☐ Environment was too dark ☐ Environment was visually under-stimulating |
| Peer context before behaviour | ☐ Peer/reacted to student ☐ Peer/s entered room<br>☐ Student bullied peer/s ☐ Peer/s moved away<br>☐ Peer/s bullied student ☐ Peer/s denied student request<br>☐ Peer/s touched student ☐ Peer/s ignored student<br>☐ Peer/s touched student's belongings ☐ Peer/s gave low levels of attention<br>☐ Peer/s reacted to student ☐ Peer/s gave high levels of attention<br>☐ Peer/s left room |

| Adult context before behaviour | **Adult present**<br>☐ Unfamiliar adult present     ☐ Non-preferred adult present<br>☐ Regular adult absent |
|---|---|
| | **Adult attention**<br>☐ Moved away     ☐ Touched student     ☐ Gave low levels of attention<br>☐ Moved closer     ☐ Ignored student     ☐ Gave high levels of attention<br>☐ Gave others attention |
| | **Adult communication**<br>☐ Asked a question suddenly     ☐ Insisted on having the last word<br>☐ Gave inconsistent directions     ☐ Brought up unrelated events<br>☐ Gave unclear directions     ☐ Made unsubstantiated accusations<br>☐ Gave complex directions     ☐ Attacked character<br>☐ Denied student request     ☐ Used unwarranted physical force<br>☐ Offered assistance without asking     ☐ Mimicked student<br>☐ Offered praise     ☐ Used tense body language<br>☐ Used sarcasm     ☐ Said 'no', 'not to', 'stop', 'don't' or 'wait'<br>☐ Used negative tone of voice<br>☐ Raised voice     ☐ Used degrading, insulting, humiliating or embarrassing put downs<br>☐ Asked student to wait<br>☐ Backed student into a corner     ☐ Gave student corrective feedback |
| Activity context before behaviour | ☐ Not applicable     ☐ Activity was difficult<br>☐ Requested activity denied     ☐ Activity was easy<br>☐ Preferred activity stopped     ☐ Activity was long<br>☐ Disliked activity was offered     ☐ Activity was repetitive<br>☐ Activity started late     ☐ Activity involved group work<br>☐ Activity finished early     ☐ Activity had many transitions<br>☐ Activity flow was interrupted     ☐ Activity involved long waiting periods<br>☐ Activity had unexpected changes<br>☐ Activity was unstructured     ☐ Activity had insufficient equipment<br>☐ Activity was unfamiliar<br>☐ Activity had no decision making opportunities     ☐ Information about upcoming activity was not given<br>☐ Activity had many decision making opportunities     ☐ Activity transition(s) occurred without sufficient warning<br>☐ Activity involved independent work     ☐ Activity transition(s) were rushed |

| | |
|---|---|
| Adult context before behaviour | **Tactile (touch) aspects**<br>☐ Activity involved too much touch<br>☐ Activity involved insufficient touch<br>☐ Activity involved unexpected touch<br>☐ Student's clothing seemed uncomfortable<br>☐ Activity item involved preferred touch<br>☐ Student's seating equipment seemed uncomfortable |
| | **Visual aspect**<br>☐ Activity included preferred visual tasks<br>☐ Activity included small font and size<br>☐ Activity had too much visual information<br>☐ Activity included non-preferred visual tasks |
| | **Olfactory (smell) aspect**<br>☐ Activity included items with a strong odour<br>☐ Activity included items with non-preferred odour<br>☐ Activity included items with preferred odour |
| | **Auditory aspect**<br>☐ Equipment was too loud<br>☐ Activity included too much auditory information<br>☐ Activity interrupted by sudden loud noises<br>☐ Activity included non-preferred auditory elements<br>☐ Activity included preferred auditory elements |
| | **Proprioceptive (body awareness) aspect**<br>☐ Activity required postural control<br>☐ Activity did not provide sufficient heavy work/resistive input<br>☐ Activity had complex motor planning/control and body awareness tasks |
| | **Gustatory (taste) aspects**<br>☐ Activity included items with non-preferred taste<br>☐ Activity included items with preferred taste<br>☐ Activity involved engaging with food items<br>☐ Activity included preferred non-food items |
| | **Vestibular (movement) aspects**<br>☐ Activity included non-preferred movement tasks<br>☐ Activity did not include movement tasks<br>☐ Activity included preferred movement tasks<br>☐ Activity included too many movement tasks |

*Positive Behaviour Support Strategies for Students with Anxious Behaviour*

# TASK 3: FBA ↦ COMPLETE 'ANALYSE INCIDENT' ↦ BEHAVIOUR

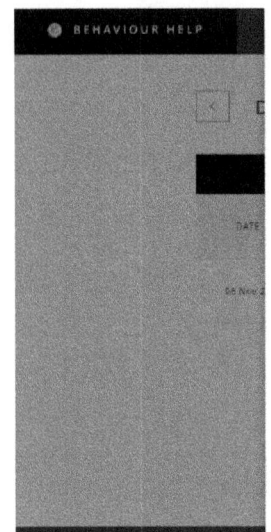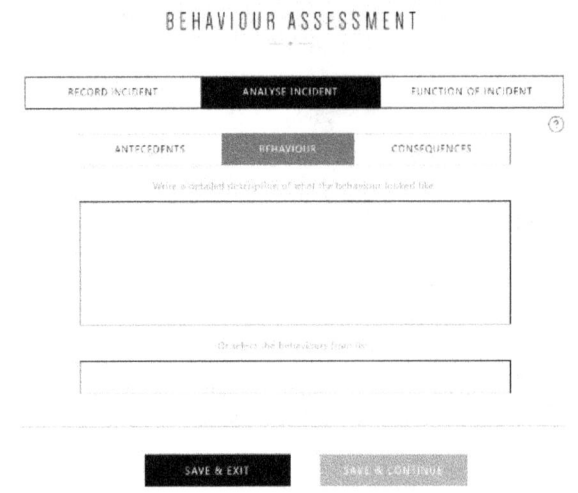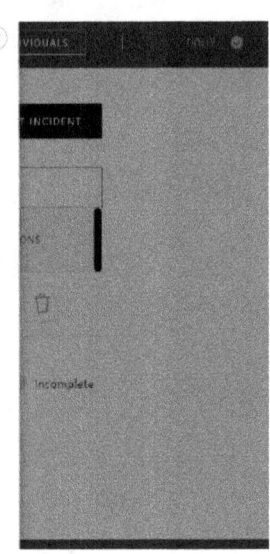

| | |
|---|---|
| WHAT? | Provide a description of the student's behaviour during the incident in observable and measurable terms. |
| WHY? | Describing behaviour in these terms instead of a vague description will allow others who were not present to have a clear picture of what the behaviour looked like. |
| HOW? | With the help of your team, write a detailed description of what the behaviour looked like. The student may exhibit externalised behaviours (signals/symptoms) that are directed towards the external environment and/or internalised behaviours (signals/symptoms) that are directed towards the self. To provide an observable description of the behaviour/s please refer to the list provided on the following pages and/or click on 'Or select the behaviours from list' in the web-based app to identify the signal/symptoms. To make your description measurable write down how many times the behaviour occurred and its duration. For example, 'April threw a half-eaten apple at Daisy who was sitting on the other side of the room' or 'Matt said three inappropriate racial remarks to David'. |

# TASK 3: EXTERNALISED SIGNALS AND SYMPTOMS

| Aggressive Behaviour | Verbally aggressive behaviour<br>☐ Interrupting others  ☐ Yelling out inappropriate comments<br>☐ Threatening others  ☐ Attempting to draw people into an argument<br>☐ Swearing at others  ☐ Attempting to draw people into a power struggle<br>☐ Screaming at others |
|---|---|
| | Physically Aggressive Behaviour<br>☐ Tripping  ☐ Punching  ☐ Pinching  ☐ Scratching  ☐ Kicking<br>☐ Choking  ☐ Biting  ☐ Pushing  ☐ Hitting |
| Disorganised | ☐ Restless  ☐ Compulsive<br>☐ Overactive  ☐ Pausing between actions<br>☐ Frantic  ☐ Running away |
| Disrupted behaviour | Inappropriate social behaviour<br>☐ Spreading rumours  ☐ Laughing inappropriately<br>☐ Lying  ☐ Making prejudicial remarks:<br>☐ Teasing           o Racial  o Religious  o Sexual orientation<br>☐ Talking excessively |
| | Inappropriate sexual behaviour<br>☐ Sexual language  ☐ Sexual propositions  ☐ Public masturbation<br>☐ Indecent exposure  ☐ Peek at others' private parts<br>☐ Sexual intercourse  ☐ Rub private parts |
| Self-injurious behaviour | ☐ Banging  ☐ Biting  ☐ Burning<br>☐ Picking  ☐ Poking  ☐ Ingesting dangerous substance<br>☐ Cutting  ☐ Slapping  ☐ Inhaling dangerous substance<br>☐ Scratching  ☐ Twisting |
| Destructive behaviour | ☐ Damaging  ☐ Throwing  ☐ Smashing<br>☐ Stealing  ☐ Breaking  ☐ Burning<br>☐ Graffitiing  ☐ Overturning  ☐ Tearing |

| Repetitive self-stimulatory behaviour | Proprioceptive repetitive self-stimulatory behaviour |
|---|---|
| | ☐ Crashing into things ☐ Grinding teeth ☐ Chewing on things<br>☐ Crashing into people ☐ Biting self ☐ Slamming things |
| | Gustatory repetitive self-stimulatory behaviour |
| | ☐ Licking objects ☐ Ruminating ☐ Placing body part in mouth<br>☐ Mouthing objects ☐ Regurgitating ☐ Eating non-food items |
| | Olfactory repetitive self-stimulatory behaviour |
| | ☐ Smelling objects ☐ Sniffing people ☐ Holding nose |
| | Vestibular repetitive self-stimulatory behaviour |
| | ☐ Spinning ☐ Swinging ☐ Rocking front to back<br>☐ Pacing ☐ Tapping foot ☐ Rocking side to side<br>☐ Bouncing ☐ Flapping hands |
| | Auditory repetitive self-stimulatory behaviour |
| | ☐ Banging objects ☐ Repetitive questioning<br>☐ Snapping fingers ☐ Giggling inappropriately<br>☐ Tapping ears ☐ Saying phrases, movies quotes, song lyrics, etc.<br>☐ Humming ☐ Making loud and/or high-pitched noises<br>☐ Covering ears |
| | Visual repetitive self-stimulatory behaviour |
| | ☐ Covering eyes ☐ Flapping hands ☐ Flicking fingers<br>☐ Closing eyes ☐ Staring at lights ☐ Lining things up<br>☐ Blinking eyes ☐ Shaking things ☐ Looking sideways at things<br>☐ Pacing ☐ Throwing or dropping objects<br>☐ Spinning things ☐ Doing a task repetitively<br>☐ Twirling objects ☐ Wiggling fingers in front or at side of face<br>☐ Twirling self ☐ Tilting head while watching objects<br>☐ Spinning self ☐ Watching moving objects<br>☐ Walking in patterns ☐ Waving fingers in front or at side of face<br>☐ Excessive drawing ☐ Opening and shutting objects<br>☐ Rocking back and forth ☐ Stacking and knocking things down<br>☐ Rocking side to side |

*Positive Behaviour Support Strategies for Students with Anxious Behaviour*

| Repetitive self-stimulatory behaviour | Tactile repetitive self-stimulatory behaviour<br><br>☐ Chewing on insides of cheeks ☐ Rubbing hands<br>☐ Mouthing objects ☐ Tapping object<br>☐ Pinching self ☐ Tapping body part<br>☐ Biting self ☐ Masturbating<br>☐ Biting fingernails ☐ Rubbing skin<br>☐ Chewing fingernails ☐ Picking skin<br>☐ Chewing skin ☐ Rubbing skin with object<br>☐ Scratching skin ☐ Clapping hands<br>☐ Banging head ☐ Grabbing someone's arm with both hands<br>☐ Grinding teeth<br>☐ Spitting ☐ Rubbing clothing between fingers<br>☐ Squeezing head against arm<br>☐ Rubbing face |
|---|---|

## INTERNALISED SIGNALS AND SYMPTOMS

☐ Withdrawn  ☐ Appearing excessively shy
☐ Seeming excessively worried  ☐ Appearing sad most of the time
☐ Seeming excessively embarrassed  ☐ Engaging in socially isolating behaviours
☐ Seeming excessively fearful  ☐ Hiding under furniture
☐ Being reluctant to participate  ☐ Hiding behind furniture
☐ Being non-responsive

# TASK 3: FBA ↦ COMPLETE 'ANALYSE INCIDENT' ↦ CONSEQUENCE

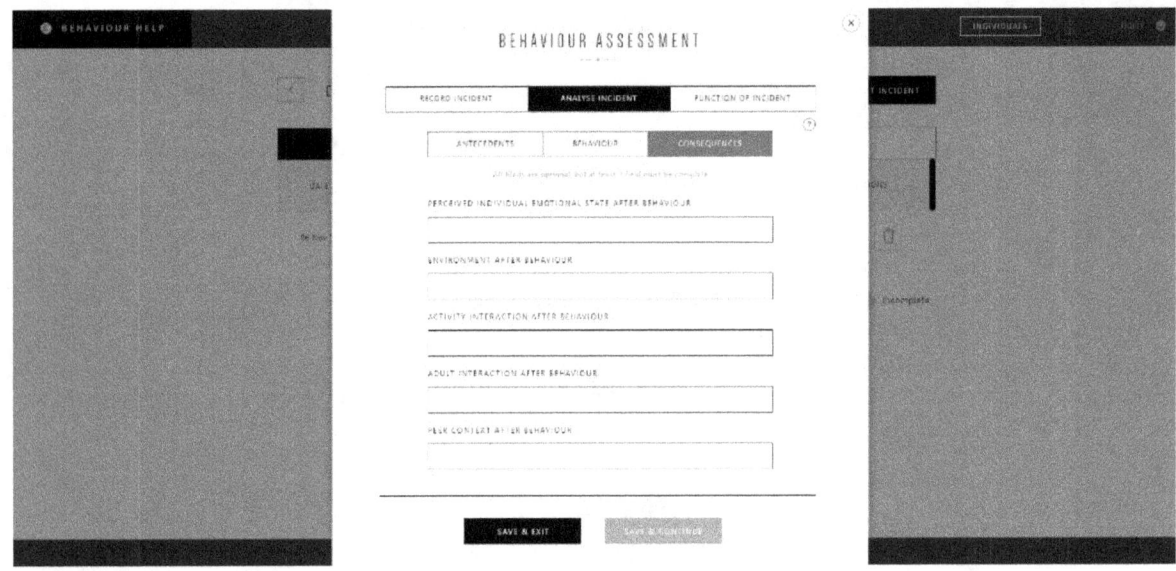

| WHAT? | Record the events (consequences) that follow the behaviour. |
|---|---|
| WHY? | This will help you understand the result of the behaviour. This information can then be used to identify intervention strategies to prevent and manage the behaviour in the future. |
| HOW? | With the help of your team, identify which of the subheadings listed on the next page and/or in the Behaviour Help web-based app refer to the consequence/s of the student's behaviour. For the selected subheadings choose the options in the drop down menu that apply and/or edit the text as appropriate. If recorded on paper, enter the information in the web-based app. |

## TASK 3: CONSEQUENCES

| | |
|---|---|
| Perceived student emotional state after behaviour | ☐ Seemed more upset     ☐ Seemed comfortable<br>☐ Seemed more worried     ☐ Seemed rested<br>☐ Seemed more agitated     ☐ Seemed safe<br>☐ Seemed more aroused     ☐ Seemed relieved<br>☐ Seemed calmer     ☐ Seemed happy<br>☐ Seemed better<br>☐ Seemed satiated<br>☐ Thirst seemed quenched |
| Environmental context after behaviour | ☐ Removed from environment     ☐ Temperature was increased<br>☐ Returned to preferred environment     ☐ Temperature was decreased |
| | Olfactory (smell) aspects<br>☐ Moved to an environment with decreased odour<br>☐ Moved to an environment with preferred odour |
| | Auditory aspects<br>☐ Moved to a quieter environment     ☐ Moved to a noisier environment |
| | Proprioceptive (body awareness) aspects<br>☐ Student offered personal space     ☐ Student moved away from others |
| | Visual aspects<br>☐ Moved to an environment with dimmer lights<br>☐ Moved to an environment with brighter lights<br>☐ Moved to an environment with less clutter<br>☐ Moved to an environment with more visual stimulation |
| Peer context after behaviour | ☐ Peer/s met request     ☐ Peer/s ignored student<br>☐ Peer/s left room     ☐ Peer/s gave higher levels of attention<br>☐ Peer/s returned to the room     ☐ Peer/s gave lower levels of attention<br>☐ Peer/s moved away     ☐ Peer/s moved away from the student<br>☐ Peer/s moved closer     ☐ Peer/s were reprimanded for bullying behaviour |
| Adult context | Adult present<br>☐ Other familiar adult entered room     ☐ Student was removed from the room |

| | |
|---|---|
| Adult context after be-haviour | **Olfactory (smell) aspects**<br>☐ Gave low levels of attention<br>☐ Gave high levels of attention<br>☐ Gave others attention<br>☐ Stopped what they were doing<br>☐ Ignored student<br>☐ Moved away<br>☐ Moved closer<br>☐ Touched student<br>☐ Preferred adult moved closer<br>☐ Left student alone<br>☐ Gave student access to preferred items |
| | **Adult communication**<br>☐ Left student alone<br>☐ Talked<br>☐ Gave clearer directions<br>☐ Gave simpler directions<br>☐ Gave requested item<br>☐ Used sarcasm<br>☐ Used negative tone of voice<br>☐ Raised voice<br>☐ Used unwarranted physical force |
| Activity context after be-haviour | ☐ Easier activity was offered<br>☐ Correct equipment was offered<br>☐ Preferred activity continued<br>☐ Preferred activity was offered<br>☐ Student worked by themselves<br>☐ Requested activity was provided<br>☐ Activity was ceased<br>☐ Student was removed from activity<br>☐ Student was offered choice of other activities |
| | **Olfactory (smell) aspect**<br>☐ Item with non-preferred odour removed<br>☐ Item with a preferred odour offered |
| | **Visual aspect**<br>☐ Offered preferred visual tasks<br>☐ Offered an activity with reduced visual content |
| | **Auditory aspect**<br>☐ Loud equipment was removed<br>☐ Moved away from loud equipment<br>☐ Offered preferred auditory items<br>☐ Auditory information in activity reduced<br>☐ Preferred auditory items offered<br>☐ Non-preferred auditory items removed |
| | **Gustatory (taste) aspects**<br>☐ Items with non-preferred taste removed<br>☐ Items with preferred taste offered<br>☐ Preferred non-edible items consumed<br>☐ Activity with food items removed |
| | **Vestibular (movement) aspects**<br>☐ Movement tasks offered ☐ Movement tasks reduced<br>☐ Movement tasks ceased |

| Activity context after behaviour | Tactile aspects<br>☐ Deep pressure touch offered<br>☐ Light pressure touch offered<br>☐ Comfortable clothing offered<br>☐ Body position changed<br>☐ Uncomfortable clothing removed<br>☐ Items with preferred touch offered<br>☐ Different seating equipment offered<br>☐ Items with non-preferred touch removed |
|---|---|

# TASK 3: FBA ↦ COMPLETE 'ANALYSE INCIDENT' ↦ INCIDENT FUNCTION

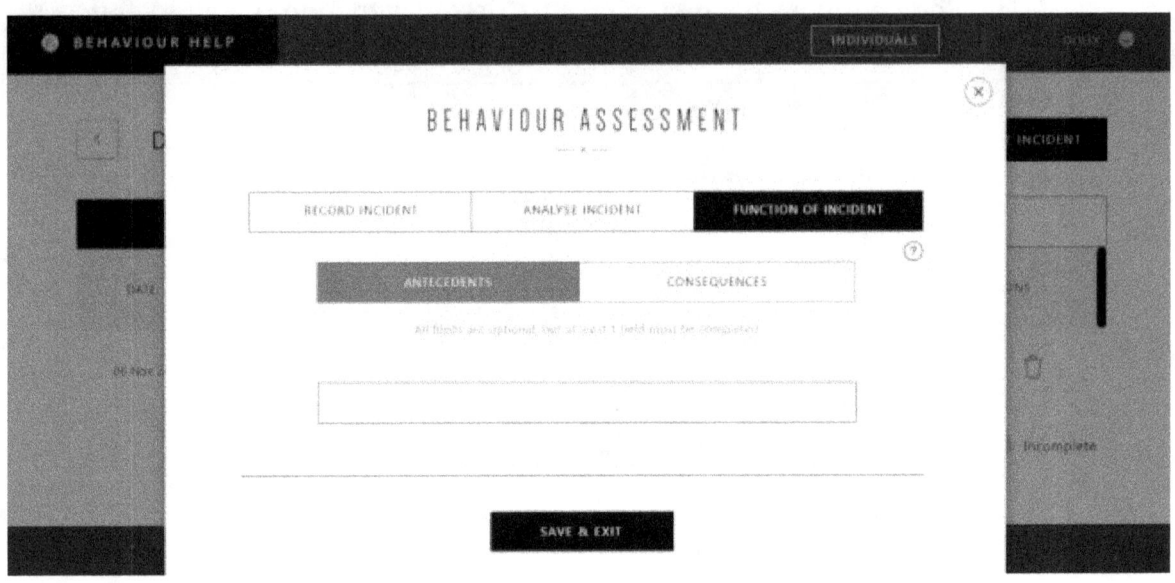

| | |
|---|---|
| WHAT? | Reflect on the antecedents (triggers) and consequences (result of the behaviour) to determine the function/s (purpose) of the behaviour. |
| WHY? | Behaviour (i.e. externalised and internalised) is communication. By understanding what the student is trying to communicate we can change either the antecedents or the consequences to prevent and manage the behaviour. |
| HOW? | With the help of your team, identify which of the subheadings listed on the next page and/or in the Behaviour Help web-based app describe the function/s. For the selected subheadings select the options using the drop down menu that apply and/or edit the text as appropriate. If recorded on paper, enter the information in the web-based app. |

# TASK 3: INCIDENT FUNCTIONS

| | |
|---|---|
| Get/obtain an object or activity | The student engages in behaviour to receive an object or participate in an activity. |
| Escape/avoid an object or activity | The student engages in behaviour to get out of receiving an object or participating in an activity. |
| Get/obtain adult attention | The student engages in behaviour to gain positive or negative social attention or reaction from an adult. |
| Escape/avoid adult attention | The student engages in behaviour to get away from positive or negative social attention or reaction from an adult. |
| Get/obtain peer attention | The student engages in behaviour to gain some form of positive or negative social attention or reaction from a peer. |
| Escape/avoid peer attention | The student engages in behaviour to get away from positive or negative social attention or reaction from a peer. |
| Get/obtain sensory input or stimulation | The student engages in behaviour to gain some form of sensory input or stimulation (i.e. visual, auditory, olfactory, gustatory, tactile, vestibular or proprioceptive). |
| Escape/avoid sensory stimulation | The student engages in behaviour to get out of receiving some form of sensory input or stimulation. |
| Get/obtain power | The student engages in behaviour to make or prevent things from happening. |
| Escape/avoid power | The student engages in behaviour to get away from having the ability to make or prevent things from happening. |
| Get/obtain influence | The student engages in behaviour to direct the behaviours of others from doing or not doing something. |
| Escape/avoid influence | The student engages in behaviour to get away from the ability to direct the behaviours of others from doing or not doing something. |
| Get/obtain status | The student engages in behaviour to get a rank or position. |
| Escape/avoid status | The student engages in behaviour to get away from obtaining a rank or position. |
| Get/obtain control | The student engages in behaviour to direct the course of events. |
| Escape/avoid control | The student engages in behaviour to get away from the ability to direct the course of events. |
| Get/obtain revenge | The student engages in behaviour to avenge the perceived or real hurt or harm caused by someone else. |

# POSITIVE BEHAVIOUR SUPPORT STRATEGIES: MANAGE STAGE

Once the function (purpose) of the target behaviour has been established, the next stage in the journey is to manage.

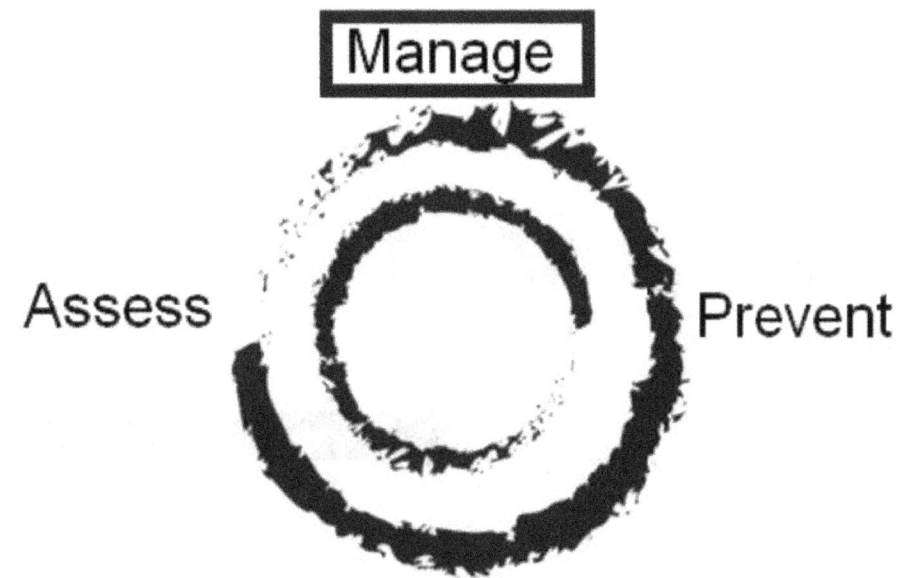

**Manage stage aim**

The Manage stage aims to develop a plan that:

1. Help those supporting the student to recognise the student's Escalation Profile (i.e. mild escalation, moderate escalation, extreme escalation and recovery stage).
2. Providing guidelines to help those supporting the student to cope with the target behaviour when it occurs in a way that it can be safely brought under control.
3. Avoid the escalation of the student's behaviour.

## Manage Stage Checklist

The Manage Stage requires you to work through the checklist tasks listed below with your transformative journey team.

Task 1 Escalation Stages

Task 2 Profile Escalation

Task 3 Manage Escalation

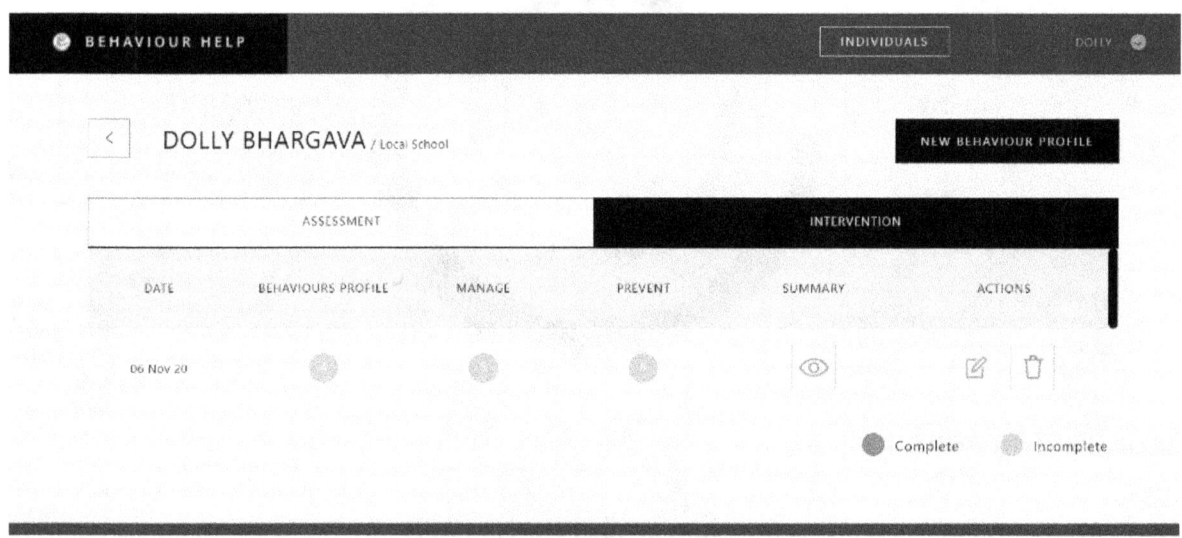

*To get started go to the Behaviour Help web-based app click on the intervention tab and then click on new behaviour profile.*

*Positive Behaviour Support Strategies for Students with Anxious Behaviour*

# TASK 1: ESCALATION STAGES

As a student's level of anger, stress and frustration increases, their behaviour escalates. This escalation can be charted in stages, i.e. mild escalation stage (low anger/stress/frustration), moderate escalation stage (medium anger/stress/frustration), extreme escalation stage (high anger/stress/frustration) and recovery stage (calming down). We are all unique and, as such, each student experiences escalation stages differently and may go through all or only some stages. To chart the Escalation Stages for your student, identify and select the number of stages your student experiences with the help of your team (e.g. four, three or two stages) in the Behaviour Help web-based app.

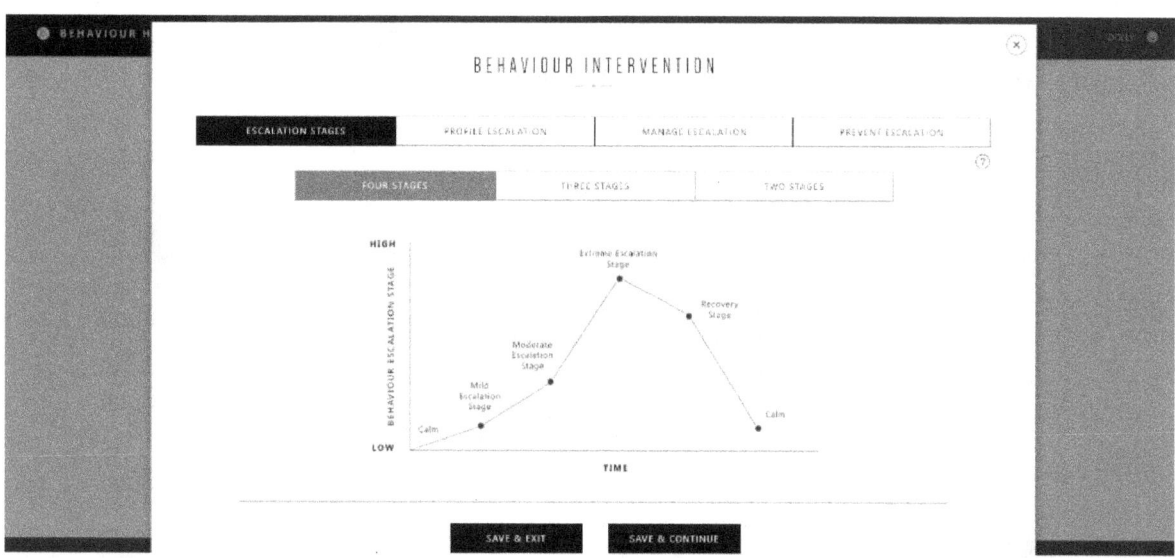

# TASK 2: PROFILE ESCALATION

Now that you have charted the number of escalations stages the student experiences, the next step is to identify the signals/symptoms the student exhibits in each stage. The student may exhibit externalised signals/symptoms (i.e. emotional and behavioural difficulties that are directed towards the external environment) and/or internalised signals/symptoms (i.e. emotional and behavioural difficulties that are directed towards the self).

To develop a Profile Escalation Plan with your team, identify and select the externalised and/or internalised signals/symptoms the student exhibits in each stage from the information listed on the follow pages and/or in the Behaviour Help web-based app. Select and enter the signals/symptoms under each escalation stage heading in the space provided in the app.

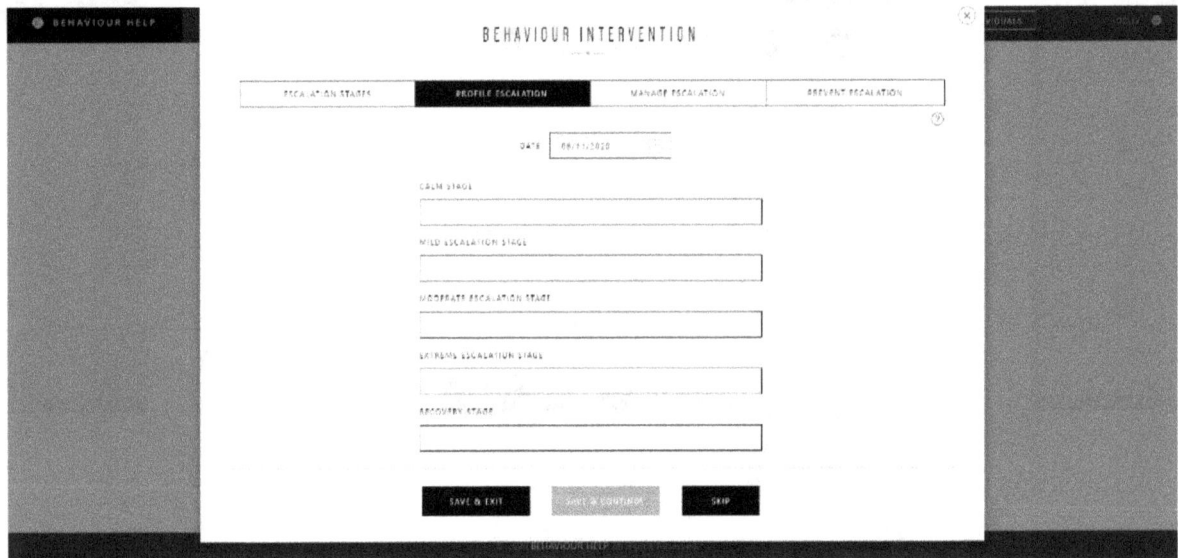

# TASK 3: MANAGE ESCALATION PLAN

This task involves working as a team to identify stage-specific strategies, i.e. mild escalation stage de-escalation strategies, moderate escalation stage de-escalation strategies, extreme escalation stage de-escalation strategies and recovery stage de-escalation strategies. This will enable everyone to take charge of the situation by safely bringing it under control, and avoid further escalation of the student's behaviour in consistent ways. To develop a Manage Escalation Plan for the student, discuss the strategies listed on the following pages and/or in the Behaviour Help web-based app with your team. Select the strategies and/ or enter the information under each escalation stage heading in the space provided in the app. Not all strategies will suit your context or meet your particular student's needs, so select and edit them as appropriate.

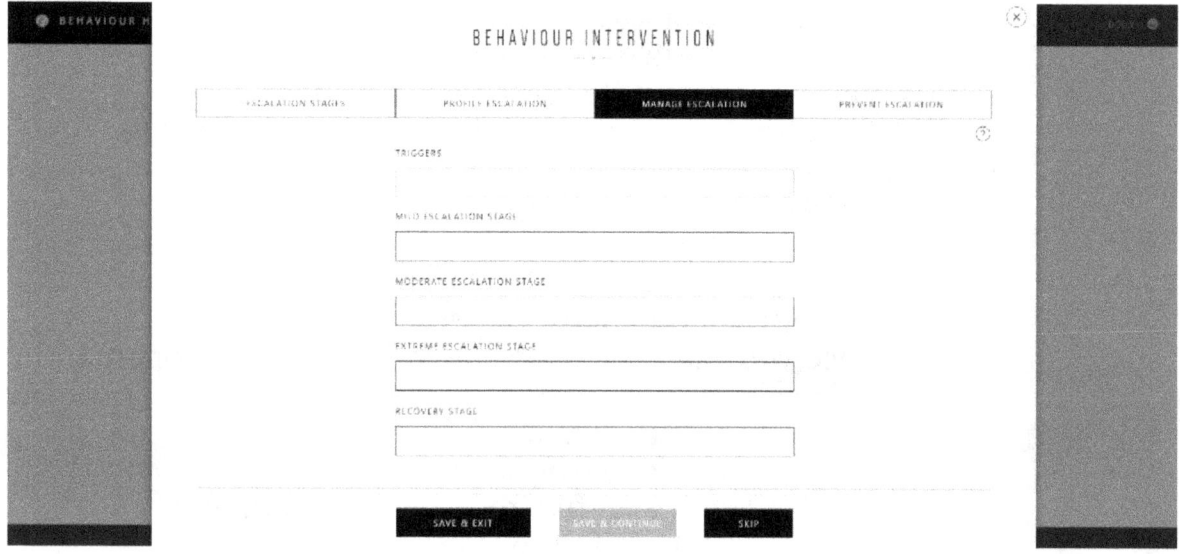

# TASK 3: MANAGE ESCALATION PLAN ↦ STAGE-SPECIFIC DE-ESCALATION STRATEGIES MILD ESCALATION STAGE ↦ DE-ESCALATION BODY LANGUAGE STRATEGIES ↦ DOS AND DON'TS

| | |
|---|---|
| WHAT? | As a parent, teacher, support staff or professional, project calm, relaxed and positive body language. |
| WHY? | Staying calm will help you think clearly and make better decisions and responses. A calm demeanour will convey to the student that you are trying to support them and not trying to threaten them, which will help them calm down. |
| HOW? | ▢ Do take deep breaths<br>▢ Do maintain a neutral facial expression<br>▢ Do maintain a safe distance from the student<br>▢ Do stand up straight with head up, feet about shoulder width apart and weight evenly balanced (if standing)<br>▢ Do appear calm and relaxed<br>▢ Do make eye contact from time to time<br>▢ Do minimise sudden body movements<br>▢ Do place your hands in front of your body in an open and relaxed position<br>▢ Do not hover over the student<br>▢ Do not use tense body language<br>▢ Do not stand with your full front facing the student<br>▢ Do not turn your back to the student<br>▢ Do not pace, fidget or shift your weight<br>▢ Do not cross arms, place hands on hips, hands in pockets or arms behind back<br>▢ Do not point or shake your finger at the student<br>▢ Do not use aggressive facial expressions or smile |

# TASK 3: MILD ESCALATION STAGE ↦ DE-ESCALATION BODY LANGUAGE STRATEGIES ↦ DOS AND DON'TS

| | |
|---|---|
| WHAT? | As a parent, teacher, support staff or professional, communicate in a respectful, non-threatening and assertive manner. |
| WHY? | Communicating in this manner will convey your confidence and authority, which will help the student calm down. |
| HOW? | ☐ Do ensure that one person communicates with the student at a time<br>☐ Do lower the volume and pitch of your voice<br>☐ Do keep your tone even and firm<br>☐ Do slow down the rate of your speech<br>☐ Do use short sentences and pause between them<br>☐ Do validate the student's feelings<br>☐ Do use 'I' messages instead of 'you' messages to state how the student's behaviour affects your thoughts and emotions<br>☐ Do state what you want the student to do instead of what you do not want them to do<br>☐ Do help the student remain focused on the main issue<br>☐ Do not have several staff communicating with the student at the same time<br>☐ Do not raise your voice, yell or scream at the student<br>☐ Do not make assumptions<br>☐ Do not respond to unrelated topics<br>☐ Do not argue, judge, interrupt or deny what the student says<br>☐ Do not insult, criticise or shame the student<br>☐ Do not use negatives such as 'no', 'don't you ever', 'no you cannot', 'don't you dare' or 'stop' |

# TASK 3: MILD ESCALATION STAGE ↦ DE-ESCALATION BODY LANGUAGE STRATEGIES ↦ REVIEW SOCIAL INTERACTION

## STRATEGICALLY IGNORE

| | |
|---|---|
| WHAT? | As a parent, teacher, support staff or professional, deliberately ignore behaviour/s that are non-threatening and attention seeking verbally and non-verbally for up to 90 seconds. |
| WHY? | By strategically ignoring non-threatening and attention seeking behaviour/s for up to 90 seconds you can avoid reinforcing the behaviour by giving it negative attention. For many students it does not matter if the attention is positive or negative, as long as they receive attention. |
| HOW? | ☐ Start strategically ignoring the behaviour immediately when it starts<br>☐ Ignore the behaviour non-verbally (e.g. do not look, give subtle glances, smile or frown) and verbally (e.g. do not talk to the student) for up to 90 seconds and/or move away from the student for up to 90 seconds |

## REINFORCE POSITIVE BEHAVIOURS

| | |
|---|---|
| WHAT? | As a parent, teacher, support staff or professional, provide reinforcement (e.g. praise, reward) when the appropriate behaviour is displayed. |
| WHY? | Reinforcing positive and appropriate behaviours provides encouragement for the good behaviour to continue for longer or more often. This can be done by reinforcing the peer/s near the student for engaging in the desired and appropriate behaviour to motivate the student to stop engaging in their inappropriate behaviour and exhibit the appropriate behaviour. However, this is not suitable for all students and can make the situation worse. In such circumstances it is more effective to purposefully look for positive behaviours the student is engaging in and then provide reinforcement. |
| HOW? | ☐ Reinforce peers engaging in appropriate behaviour<br>☐ Reinforce the student for engaging in appropriate behaviour |

## RULE REMINDER

| WHAT? | As a parent, teacher, support staff or professional, remind the student about the rules. |
|---|---|
| WHY? | Stating the rule reminds the student of what you want them to do rather than what you do not want them to do. |
| HOW? | ☐ Remind peers of the rules<br>☐ Make eye contact with the student to indicate awareness of behaviour<br>☐ Use non-verbal cues or signals to remind the student to stop the behaviour<br>☐ Move closer to the student, quietly remind them of what you want them to do and say 'thank you' or 'thanks' at end of the rule<br>☐ Move away to give student time and space to process and decide to comply with instruction |

## CONSEQUENCE REMINDER

| WHAT? | As a parent, teacher, support staff or professional, state the consequences of misbehaviour and rewards of appropriate behaviour. |
|---|---|
| WHY? | Stating consequences reminds the student that their actions have outcomes and helps them reflect on their choices. |
| HOW? | ☐ Remind peers of the rewards for behaving appropriately and the consequences of behaving inappropriately<br>☐ Alternatively, move closer to the student and quietly remind them of the reward for behaving ppropriately<br>☐ Move away to give the student time and space to process and comply with the instruction<br>☐ If the student does not comply, remind them of the rule, restate the consequences and move away |

## FOLLOW THROUGH WITH CONSEQUENCE

| | |
|---|---|
| WHAT? | As a parent, teacher, support staff or professional, enforce what you have said by following through with the consequence. |
| WHY? | By consistently following through with your stated consequence the student will trust that you will do as you say. |
| HOW? | ☐ If the student engages in misbehaviour after repeated warning, impose loss of reward<br>☐ If the student engages in misbehaviour after repeated warning, impose loss of privilege<br>☐ If the student engages in misbehaviour after repeated warning, impose time out<br>☐ If the student engages in misbehaviour after repeated warning, impose detention |

# TASK 3: MILD ESCALATION STAGE ↦ DE-ESCALATION BODY LANGUAGE STRATEGIES ↦ REVIEW ACTIVITY

## OFFER HELP

| | |
|---|---|
| WHAT? | As a parent, teacher, support staff or professional, help the student participate in an activity. |
| WHY? | Offering help informs the student that you are there to assist and it is their choice to accept or reject help. |
| HOW? | ☐ Move closer to the student<br>☐ Ask if the student would like help with the activity<br>☐ If the student does not accept offer, acknowledge and move away<br>☐ If the student accepts offer, acknowledge and provide assistance |

## DEAL WITH THE PROBLEMATIC ACTIVITY TOGETHER

| | |
|---|---|
| WHAT? | As a parent, teacher, support staff or professional, work with the student, to identify the problem and possible solutions. |
| WHY? | By working together makes the problem solving process less threatening and ensures that the student feels heard. |
| HOW? | ☐ Speak to the student privately<br>☐ Speak slowly in a calm, low and monotonous voice<br>☐ Ask the student to talk about the problem<br>☐ Actively listen to the student<br>☐ Acknowledge feelings by empathising with the student<br>☐ Discuss possible solutions with the student<br>☐ Choose the most effective solution collaboratively |

## MODIFY ACTIVITY

| WHAT? | As a parent, teacher, support staff or professional, adjust the activity so that the student can overcome the difficulty. |
|---|---|
| WHY? | Adjusting the activity can reduce the student's confusion, frustration and upset. |
| HOW? | ☐ Alter level of difficulty<br>☐ Alter length<br>☐ Alter time provided<br>☐ Alter outcome<br>☐ Alter level of participation<br>☐ Alter content<br>☐ Alter materials<br>☐ Alter activity to include sensory input to meet sensory craving |

# TASK 3: MILD ESCALATION STAGE ↦ DE-ESCALATION BODY LANGUAGE STRATEGIES ↦ REVIEW ENVIRONMENT

| WHAT? | As a parent, teacher, support staff or professional, reduce the demands of the environment. |
|---|---|
| WHY? | Adjusting or giving the student a break from the environment can help them calm down. |
| HOW? | ☐ Adjust sensory stimulation in environment<br>☐ Ask the student to move to a different environment<br>☐ Provide increased personal space |

# TASK 3: MANAGE ESCALATION PLAN ↪ STAGE-SPECIFIC DE-ESCALATION STRATEGIES ↪ MODERATE ESCALATION STAGE ↪ DE-ESCALATION BODY LANGUAGE STRATEGIES ↪ DOs AND DON'Ts

| | |
|---|---|
| WHAT? | As a parent, teacher, support staff or professional, project calm, relaxed and positive body language. |
| WHY? | Staying calm will help you think clearly and make better decisions and responses. Your calm demeanour will convey to the student that you are trying to support them and not trying to threaten them, which will help them calm down. |
| HOW? | ☐ Do take deep breaths<br>☐ Do maintain a neutral facial expression<br>☐ Do maintain a safe distance from the student<br>☐ Do stand up straight with head up, feet about shoulder width apart and weight evenly balanced (if standing)<br>☐ Do appear calm and relaxed<br>☐ Do position yourself closer to the room entrance so you can make a quick exit if required<br>☐ Do stand or sit at an angle or alongside the student so you can sidestep away if necessary<br>☐ Do make eye contact from time to time<br>☐ Do minimise sudden body movements<br>☐ Do place your hands in front of your body in an open and relaxed position<br>☐ Do not hover over the student<br>☐ Do not use tense body language<br>☐ Do not allow the student to block your exit from the room<br>☐ Do not stand with your full front facing the student<br>☐ Do not turn your back to the student<br>☐ Do not pace, fidget or shift your weight<br>☐ Do not cross arms, place hands on hips, hands in pockets or arms behind back |

# TASK 3: DE-ESCALATION REDIRECTION STRATEGIES ↦ DOS AND DON'TS

| | |
|---|---|
| WHAT? | As a parent, teacher, support staff or professional, communicate in a respectful, non-threatening and non-confrontational manner. |
| WHY? | Communicating in this manner will convey your confidence and authority, which will help the student calm down. |
| HOW? | ☐ Do engage in minimal talking<br>☐ Do ensure that if instructions have to be given they are kept short and simple<br>☐ State the instruction as a positive (do statement) rather than a negative (don't statement)<br>☐ Offer student choices 'you can do this ... or this ...'<br>☐ Do speak slowly in a calm, low and monotonous voice<br>☐ Do use the student's name<br>☐ Do ignore and disregard the student's inappropriate language<br>☐ Do not raise your voice, yell or scream at the student<br>☐ Do not make assumptions<br>☐ Do not argue, judge, interrupt or deny what the student says<br>☐ Do not insult, criticise or shame the student |

# TASK 3: DE-ESCALATION REDIRECTION STRATEGIES ↪ REVIEW SOCIAL INTERACTION

## USE SOCIAL DISTRACTION

| | |
|---|---|
| **WHAT?** | As a parent, teacher, support staff or professional, direct the student's attention to something else. |
| **WHY?** | Giving the student something else to do or think about can help them stop focusing on what is agitating, upsetting or frustrating and direct them toward something pleasant. |
| **HOW?** | ☐ Use humour<br>☐ Change topic of conversation<br>☐ Use unusual noises or movements to obtain the student's attention<br>☐ Ask student to help someone else<br>☐ Change peer/s interacting with the student<br>☐ Change adult interacting with the student |

## REDUCE SOCIAL DEMANDS

| | |
|---|---|
| **WHAT?** | As a parent, teacher, support staff or professional, give the student a break from the social situation until they have calmed down sufficiently. |
| **WHY?** | Moving the student to a different area provides them with the opportunity to have a break from the person that may be agitating them, regroup and calm down. |
| **HOW?** | ☐ Prompt the student to move away from instigating peers<br>☐ Prompt peers to move away from the student<br>☐ Prompt peers to minimise interaction with the student<br>☐ Prompt other adult/s to minimise interaction with the student<br>☐ Prompt the student to move closer to a particular adult |

# TASK 3: DE-ESCALATION REDIRECTION STRATEGIES ↪ REVIEW ACTIVITY

| WHAT? | As a parent, teacher, support staff or professional, direct the student's attention to a different activity. |
|---|---|
| WHY? | Giving the student something else to do or think about can help them to stop focusing on what is agitating, upsetting or frustrating and direct them toward something pleasant. |
| HOW? | ☐ Prompt the student to stop routine activity<br>☐ Offer choice between preferred activity/s<br>☐ Offer sensory activity/s<br>☐ Offer physical activity/s<br>☐ Offer relaxation activity/s<br>☐ Ask the student to run an errand |

## TASK 3: DE-ESCALATION REDIRECTION STRATEGIES ↪ REVIEW ENVIRONMENT

| WHAT? | As a parent, teacher, support staff or professional, direct the student to a different environment. |
|---|---|
| WHY? | Moving the student to a different environment can help them to stop focusing on what is agitating, upsetting or frustrating them and direct them toward something pleasant. |
| HOW? | ☐ Prompt the student to go for a walk<br>☐ Prompt the student to go to a calm down area<br>☐ Prompt the student to go to the sensory room<br>☐ Prompt the student to go to a different environment |

# TASK 3: MANAGE ESCALATION PLAN ↪ STAGE-SPECIFIC DE-ESCALATION STRATEGIES ↪ EXTREME ESCALATION STAGE ↪ DE-ESCALATION BODY LANGUAGE STRATEGIES ↪ DOS AND DON'TS

| WHAT? | As a parent, teacher, support staff or professional, project calm, relaxed and positive body language. |
|---|---|
| WHY? | Staying calm will help you think clearly, make better decisions and responses. A calm demeanour will convey to the student that you are trying to support them and not trying to threaten them, which will help them calm down. |
| HOW? | ☐ Do appear calm and relaxed<br>☐ Do keep a safe distance<br>☐ Do give no eye contact<br>☐ Do not use tense body language<br>☐ Do not stare<br>☐ Do not turn your back to the student<br>☐ Do not touch the student<br><br>☐ Do not pace, fidget or shift your weight<br>☐ Do not allow the student to block your exit from the room<br>☐ Do not cross arms, place hands on hips, hands in pockets or arms behind back<br>☐ Do not point or shake your finger at the student<br>☐ Do not use aggressive facial expressions or smile<br>☐ Do not stand with your full front facing the student |

# TASK 3: EXTREME ESCALATION STAGE ↦ DE-ESCALATION LANGUAGE STRATEGIES ↦ DOS AND DON'TS

| WHAT? | As a parent, teacher, support staff or professional, communicate in a respectful, non-threatening and assertive manner. |
|---|---|
| WHY? | Communicating in this manner will convey your confidence and authority, which will help the student calm down. |
| HOW? | ☐ Do engage in minimal or no talking<br>☐ Do ensure that if instructions have to be given they are kept short and simple<br>☐ Do speak slowly in a calm, low and monotonous voice<br>☐ Do use the student's name<br>☐ Do ignore and disregard the student's inappropriate language<br>☐ Do not raise your voice, yell or scream at the student<br>☐ Do not argue, judge, interrupt or deny what the student says<br>☐ Do not insult, criticise or shame the student<br>☐ Do not discipline during this stage |

# TASK 3: EXTREME ESCALATION STAGE ↦ DE-ESCALATION REDIRECTION STRATEGIES ↦ PROTECT STAFF AND PEERS

| WHAT? | As a parent, teacher, support staff or professional, direct the people around the student to a safe place. |
|---|---|
| WHY? | To ensure the safety and well-being of everyone around the student. |
| HOW? | ☐ Send others away from the location |

# TASK 3: EXTREME ESCALATION STAGE ↦ DE-ESCALATION REDIRECTION STRATEGIES ↦ PROTECT STUDENT

| WHAT? | As a parent, teacher, support staff or professional, direct the student to a safe place. |
|---|---|
| WHY? | To ensure the safety and well-being of the student. |
| HOW? | ☐ Provide the student with space<br>☐ Allow the student time to rage it out<br>☐ Prompt the student to go to a calm down area<br>☐ Physically move the student to a safe location<br>☐ Use physical restraint as advised in policy guidelines<br>☐ Remove potentially harmful objects |

# TASK 3: MANAGE ESCALATION PLAN ↦ STAGE-SPECIFIC DE-ESCALATION STRATEGIES ↦ RECOVERY STAGE ↦ DE-ESCALATION BODY LANGUAGE STRATEGIES ↦ DOS AND DON'TS

| WHAT? | As a parent, teacher, support staff or professional, project a calm, relaxed and positive body language. | |
|---|---|---|
| WHY? | Staying calm will help you think clearly, and make better decisions and responses. A calm demeanour will convey to the student that you are trying to support them and not trying to threaten or challenge them, which will help them calm down. | |
| HOW? | ☐ Do take time to regroup<br>☐ Do appear calm and relaxed<br>☐ Do not stare<br>☐ Do keep a safe distance from the student<br>☐ Do give eye contact from time to time<br>☐ Do not use tense body language<br>☐ Do not pace, fidget or shift your weight | ☐ Do not turn your back to the student<br>☐ Do not point or shake your finger at the student<br>☐ Do not use aggressive facial expressions or smile<br>☐ Do not stand with your full front facing the student<br>☐ Do not cross arms, place hands on hips, hands in pockets or arms behind back |

# TASK 3: RECOVERY STAGE ↦ DE-ESCALATION LANGUAGE STRATEGIES ↦ DOS AND DON'TS

| WHAT? | As a parent, teacher, support staff or professional, communicate in a respectful, non-threatening and assertive manner. |
|---|---|
| WHY? | Communicating in this manner it will convey your confidence and authority, which will help the student calm down. |
| HOW? | ☐ Do engage in minimal talking<br>☐ Do not refer to the episode<br>☐ Do not discipline the student<br>☐ Do not embarrass the student<br>☐ Do not blame the student<br>☐ Do not force the student to apologise<br>☐ Do use the student's name<br><br>☐ Do give instructions that are short and simple<br>☐ Do speak slowly in a calm, low and monotonous voice<br>☐ Do respond if the student initiates conversation<br>☐ Do empathise with and listen to the student<br>☐ Do not raise your voice, yell or scream at the student<br>☐ Do not talk about how the behaviour hurt others' feelings |

# TASK 3: RECOVERY STAGE ↦ DE-ESCALATION REDIRECTION STRATEGIES ↦ REVIEW ACTIVITY

| WHAT? | As a parent, teacher, support staff or professional, adjust the activity demands. |
|---|---|
| WHY? | Gradually increasing the demands can help the student participate in activities and experience success. |
| HOW? | ☐ Be aware that recovery can take up to 45 minutes<br>☐ Ask the student periodically if they are ready to engage in an activity<br>☐ If the student is not ready, continue to give space<br>☐ If the student is ready, offer a sensory activity<br>☐ If the student is ready, offer an activity based on a special interest<br>☐ If the student is ready, direct them to a routine activity that is familiar and easy<br>☐ Gradually re-introduce more challenging routine activities |

## TASK 3: RECOVERY STAGE ↦ DE-ESCALATION REDIRECTION STRATEGIES ↦ REVIEW ENVIRONMENT

| | |
|---|---|
| WHAT? | As a parent, teacher, support staff or professional, adjust the environmental demands. |
| WHY? | Gradually increasing the environmental demands can help the student feel safe and able to cope in the environment. |
| HOW? | ☐ Be aware that recovery can take up to 45 minutes<br>☐ Ask the student periodically if they are ready to re-enter routine environment<br>☐ If the student is not ready, continue to give space<br>☐ If the student is ready, provide support to re-enter routine environment |

# TASK 3 RECOVERY STAGE ↦ DE-ESCALATION RE-DIRECTION STRATEGIES ↦ REVIEW SOCIAL INTERACTION

| | |
|---|---|
| WHAT? | As a parent, teacher, support staff or professional, adjust the social demands. |
| WHY? | Gradually increasing the social demands can help the student participate in social interaction and experience success. |
| HOW? | ☐ Be aware that recovery can take up to 45 minutes<br>☐ Ask the student periodically if they are ready to engage with peers<br>☐ If the student is not ready, continue to give space<br>☐ If the student is ready, provide support to re-engage with supportive peers<br>☐ Supervise the student's interaction with peers<br>☐ Seat the student closer to a particular adult<br>☐ Seat the student away from a particular adult |

# POSITIVE BEHAVIOUR SUPPORT STRATEGIES: PREVENT STAGE

Once the manage stage of the target behaviour has been established, the next stage in the transformative journey is to prevent.

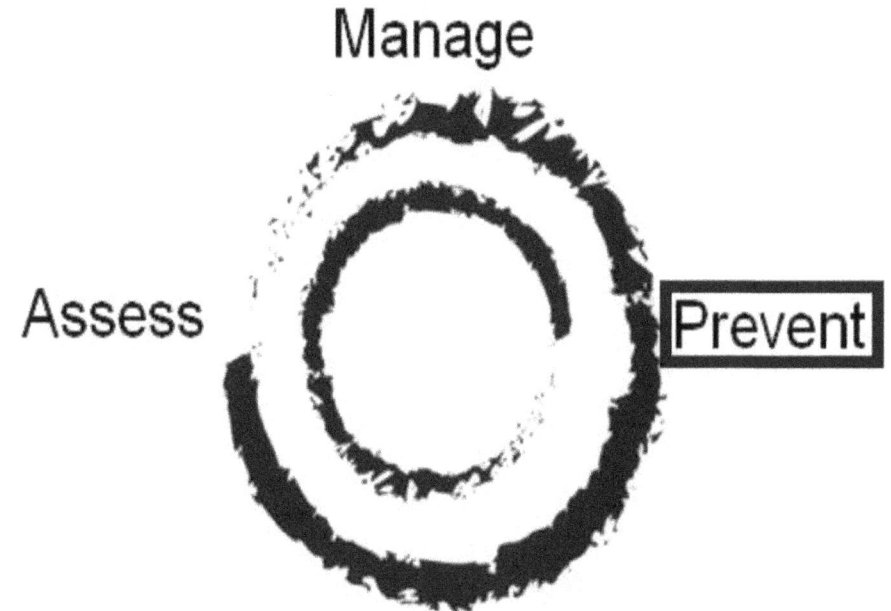

**Prevent stage aim**

The Prevent stage focuses on:

1. Minimising or avoiding the triggers that set off the target behaviour.
2. Tailoring the activity, environment and interactions with the student for successful prevention of the target behaviour.
3. Teaching the student positive ways of communicating their messages, and managing their emotions and behaviours.

**Prevent Stage Checklist**

The Prevent Stage requires you to work through the checklist task with your transformative journey team.

Task 1 Prevent Escalation

# TASK 1: PREVENT ESCALATION

The Prevent Escalation phase focuses on developing a plan that aims to minimise or avoid the triggers that set off the target behaviour; tailor the activity, environment and interactions with the student for successful prevention of the target behaviour; and teach the student positive ways of communicating their messages and managing their emotions and behaviours.

To develop the Prevent Escalation plan for the student, discuss the strategies listed on the following pages and/or in the Behaviour Help web-based app with your team. Select the strategies and/or enter the information under each Escalation Stage heading in the space provided in the app. Not all the strategies will suit your context or meet your particular student's needs, so select and edit them as appropriate.

# TASK 1: PREVENT ESCALATION ↦ ACTIVITY STRATEGIES

## ACTIVITY PARTICIPATION

| | |
|---|---|
| **WHAT?** | As a parent, teacher, support staff or professional, maintain flexible expectations of the student's level of participation from activity to activity based on their needs. |
| **WHY?** | The student may experience persistent feelings of excessive or unreasonable fear, worry or stress in the presence of or in anticipation (imagined) of a perceived threat within an activity. The overestimation of the threat and the fear of being embarrassed, humiliated or failing is so great that causes the student to withdraw or avoid the activity. Withdrawal or avoidance however only reinforces that the worries, fears and stresses were genuine and real, which in turn encourages further avoidance. Hence, by adapting the level of participation you can help the student face their fears, worry and stresses by taking really small, realistic and gradual steps. This can provide the student with the opportunity to learn that the activity can be tolerated and their fears, stresses and worries are not true. |
| **HOW?** | ☐ Have flexible expectations of participation levels from activity to activity based on the student's emotional needs<br>☐ Encourage participation in anxiety provoking activities by setting small, realistic and attainable goals<br>☐ Gradually increase level of challenge as the student's level of comfort increases.<br>☐ Level 1 – Student engages in observer participation by not actively partaking in activity<br>☐ Level 2 – Student engages in partial participation by actively partaking in one or more steps/tasks within the activity<br>☐ Level 3 – Student engages in complete participation by actively partaking in the entire activity |

# ACTIVITY VISUALS, MATERIALS AND RESOURCES

| WHAT? | As a parent, teacher, support staff or professional, use a variety of activity visuals, materials and resources to enable the student to accomplish tasks successfully. |
|---|---|
| WHY? | By using a variety of visuals listed below (e.g. daily schedule, rule chart, instruction summary, reward system and free time activity choices) you can provide predictability and certainty which can help reduce anxiety. A feelings visual can help the student keep track of the intensity or degree of their anxiety and utilise strategies to prevent its escalation. Activity visuals provide verbal information in a format that the student can access at any time without having to depend on others to verbally remind them. By providing extra materials you can ensure that the student can get on with participating in the activity instead of feeling frustrated or stalling because they have forgotten instructions. Providing resources that cater to the student's need for quiet-time breaks, physical movement breaks and assist with their comprehension, writing and spelling difficulties can motivate and support them to successfully participate in activities. Anxiety also effects the student's ability to remember so by having extra activity materials you can avoid the student worrying that they will forget to bring the material or feel embarrassed if they do. A timer can help the student understand in a tangible way exactly how long they need to persist in an activity. |
| HOW? | ☐ Daily schedule visual<br>☐ Rules chart visual<br>☐ Materials checklist visual<br>☐ Instruction summary visual<br>☐ Reward system visual<br><br>☐ Free time activity choices visual<br>☐ Feelings chart visual<br>☐ Extra activity materials for the student to borrow<br>☐ Timers to help the student focus |

# ACTIVITY DESIGN

| | |
|---|---|
| WHAT? | As a parent, teacher, support staff or professional, design activities that alternate in their demands. Additionally, tailor activities and break-time activities to match the student's needs. |
| WHY? | It is important to reward the student for being brave and coping in an activity that they perceive as being threatening. The more the student participates in the activity it will help build their frustration tolerance which is critical skills necessary for handling stressful situations. Also, by tailoring the activities by utilising the strategies listed below, you can create a fit between the student's needs and the activity demands and expectations. Structuring opportunities to do heavy work, calming down and movement activities can help the student regain and maintain their emotional control. |
| HOW? | ☐ Provide rewards that match the level of difficulty associated with the achievement of each goal<br>☐ Use cooperative learning strategies to minimise competition in activities<br>☐ Adjust difficulty of the activity so that there is a high rate of correct response to the activity<br>☐ Adjust activity length so that there is a high rate of positive engagement with the activity<br>☐ Adjust time provided to complete activity<br>☐ Adjust activity outcome based on the student's preferences, ability and needs<br>☐ Adjust activity process based on the student's preferences, ability and needs<br>☐ Adjust activity content based on the student's preferences, ability and needs<br>☐ Adjust activity visuals, materials and resources based on the student's preferences, ability and needs<br>☐ Break activity down into small and doable steps<br>☐ Identify and allocate the student with jobs or responsibilities which they can complete successfully<br>☐ Structure activities during unstructured times<br>☐ Provide opportunities for engaging in heavy work activities, calming down activities and movement activities<br>☐ especially before or after difficult activities |

## ACTIVITY INTRUCTION

| | |
|---|---|
| WHAT? | As a parent, teacher, support staff or professional, adapt the activity instruction method, reinforcement and management style to match the student's needs. |
| WHY? | By making adaptations listed below, you can carry out an activity in ways that enable the student to successfully participate in the activity from the beginning to the end. |
| HOW? | ☐ Before commencing activities ensure all the necessary activity visual aids, materials and resources are available<br>☐ Remove items that are not being used to eliminate unnecessary distractions<br>☐ Limit the number of adult supervising and facilitating the student's skill development at a time<br>☐ Maintain pace and flow by minimising time taken to present information<br>☐ Use consistent pattern for starting activities<br>☐ Gain the student's attention before giving instruction<br>☐ Speak in a varied tone, pitch, volume and inflection to emphasise and add interest<br>☐ Review rules, expectations and aim of activity<br>☐ Be aware of rate, length and complexity of information<br>☐ Use a combination of visual, auditory and kinaesthetic modes to provide instruction<br>☐ Organise instructions in sequence<br>☐ Give one instruction at a time<br>☐ Provide time to process<br>☐ Keep talking to a minimum as the student engages in the activity<br>☐ Ask if the student needs assistance and offer help accordingly<br>☐ Help the student identify and correct their own errors<br>☐ Re-frame mistakes as being a normal part of every learning experience that help us grow<br>☐ Insert stress reduction breaks at the beginning, middle and end of activities to prevent the student from becoming frustrated<br>☐ Use private and discreet signals to remind the student to re-focus on activity<br>☐ Provide advance warning that the student will be called upon shortly<br>☐ Prepare and provide explanations for any changes<br>☐ Provide advance warnings and prepare the student for transitions through a finishing routine<br>☐ Have a consistent pattern for ending activity |

*Positive Behaviour Support Strategies for Students with Anxious Behaviour*

# TASK 1: PREVENT ESCALATION ↦ INTERACTION STRATEGIES

## ADULT INTERACTION

| | |
|---|---|
| WHAT? | As a parent, teacher, support staff or professional, interact with the student in ways that demonstrate your understanding, acceptance and responsiveness to the student's needs. |
| WHY? | By interacting in ways listed below, that is mindful of the student's anxiety we can help the student feel valued, respected and supported. |
| HOW? | ☐ Get agreement on language that will be consistently used to give the student feedback<br>☐ Establish consistency in behavioural reactions, expectations and management strategies between adults<br>☐ Be consistent in your interactions, expectations and reactions<br>☐ Be approachable and friendly<br>☐ Demonstrate caring behaviour towards all students<br>☐ Show genuine interest in student<br>☐ Build a relationship by getting to know student interests, personality and background<br>☐ Strengthen student spirit, self-esteem and confidence by never shaming student<br>☐ Communicate high but realistic expectations to student that can be enforced consistently<br>☐ Build student trust by doing what you said you were going to do<br>☐ Build the student's trust by doing what you said you were going to do<br>☐ Monitor the student's anxiety<br>☐ Manage self-anxiety by limiting displays of distress<br>☐ Do not discount criticise or invalidate the student's anxiety<br>☐ Acknowledge and empathise with the student's anxiety<br>☐ Normalise anxiety as an emotion that everyone experiences<br>☐ De-stigmatise help seeking and give the student positive reinforcement for asking for help<br>☐ Model appropriate social and calm behaviour<br>☐ Provide achievement feedback by helping the student reflect on self-progress rather than comparing with peers or group<br>☐ Increase the student's ability to self-reassure by asking them to answer their own questions or concerns<br>☐ Reduce attention to anxious behaviour<br>☐ Recognise and reward the student for brave behaviour of engaging and coping in anxiety provoking situations<br>☐ Reward brave and non-anxious behaviour<br>☐ Redirect anxious behaviour by focusing on positives and successes<br>☐ Offer evidence to dispute negative perceptions<br>☐ Reframe the student's anxious comments by offering evidence to dispute negative perceptions<br>☐ Narrate the student's experience to help them remember the experience more accurately |

## PEER INTERACTION

| | |
|---|---|
| WHAT? | As a parent, teacher, support staff or professional, support positive student – peer interaction so that relationships can be built and successful teamwork can be achieved. |
| WHY? | The student experiences a range of social skill difficulties which influence their ability to build relationships and work successfully with their peers. While it is not possible to force friendships, it is possible to create opportunities that encourage friendships to develop. |
| HOW? | ☐ Consider the number of peer(s) that can do an activity with the student<br>☐ Provide peer mediation to manage disputes<br>☐ Educate peers about the student's needs<br>☐ Seat the student next to a peer study buddy who can help maintain attention<br>☐ Use a buddy system to help the student develop social relationships |

## STUDENT INTERACTION

| | |
|---|---|
| WHAT? | As a parent, teacher, support staff or professional, teach the student a range of skills systematically and explicitly. |
| WHY? | To determine if the student needs specific skills training in any of the areas listed below, contact a professional (e.g. speech pathologist, occupational therapist, psychologist) to conduct an assessment and provide intervention if appropriate. |
| HOW? | ☐ Teach the student compliance skills<br>☐ Teach the student communication skills<br>☐ Teach the student social skills<br>☐ Teach the student emotional regulation skills<br>☐ Teach the student problem solving skills<br>☐ Teach the student time management skills<br>☐ Teach the student organisational skills<br>☐ Teach the student self-regulation skills<br>☐ Teach the student cognitive flexibility skills<br>☐ Use behavioural contracts to help the student understand goal/expectations, consequences and rewards for compliance<br>☐ Use tangible rewards, edible rewards, social rewards, activity rewards and token economy to motivate the student to work towards their goal |

# TASK 1 PREVENT ESCALATION ↦ ENVIRONMENTAL STRATEGIES

## PHYSICAL ENVIRONMENT

| | |
|---|---|
| WHAT? | As a parent, teacher, support staff or professional, purposefully arrange the environment in ways that are responsive to the needs of the student. |
| WHY? | By utilising the strategies listed below, the environment can provide certainty and predictability which can help minimise the student's anxiety. Also, a distraction free environment can also help the student stay on track and avoid losing things. |
| HOW? | ☐ Create a clutter free and organised environment by using labelled storage systems to store materials<br>☐ Designate and label specific places for items to be placed<br>☐ Divide environment into activity specific areas<br>☐ Create physical and/or visual boundaries to help the student know where each activity area begins and ends<br>☐ Reduce visually distracting stimuli<br>☐ Allocate a calm down area<br>☐ Reduce auditory stimuli<br>☐ Set up environment to provide maximum personal space for everyone |

## POSITIONING IN ENVIRONMENT

| | |
|---|---|
| WHAT? | As a parent, teacher, support staff or professional, position the student in the environment in ways that are responsive to their needs. |
| WHY? | Considered positioning of the student in the environment can encourage them to be able to focus, develop skills and stay on task. |
| HOW? | ☐ Position the student near the front of the room (so they are able to see or not see peers)<br>☐ Position the student in close proximity to adult to access prompting, correction or reinforcement<br>☐ Position the student next to peers who are good role models |

## ENVIRONMENTAL ROUTINES

| | |
|---|---|
| WHAT? | As a parent, teacher, support staff or professional, create and practise routines that will foster the student's independence, sense of safety and self-confidence. |
| WHY? | Adhering to strategies listed below of establishing and following routines can provide the necessary structure to help the student stay on track, which can then help reduce anxiety related emotional and behavioural difficulties. |
| HOW? | ☐ Establish an individualised routine that matches the student's needs, abilities and preferences<br>☐ Establish and follow routine consistently<br>☐ Establish and practise routines for entering the environment<br>☐ Establish and practise routines for getting ready for the activity<br>☐ Establish and practise routines for using visuals<br>☐ Establish and practise routines for collecting materials and resources<br>☐ Establish and practise routines for moving around<br>☐ Establish and practise routines for waiting<br>☐ Establish and practise routines for leaving the environment<br>☐ Establish and practise routines for transitioning between environments<br>☐ Insert a structured chat time in the day when the student can discuss their anxieties as well as positive occurrences |

# CONCLUDING REMARK

The journey of transformation is a cyclic, ongoing process that consists of three stages: Assess – Prevent – Manage. To evaluate the effectiveness of the Manage and Prevent stages, refer to the Assess Stage Checklist → Task 2 → Target Behaviour Data Collection Forms. By collecting the frequency, intensity and duration of the target behaviour again, you can measure the amount or type of progress that has been made. This can help you determine the effectiveness of the strategies. Based on this information, you can then make adjustments to the Management and Prevention plans. To assist the student in transforming their other emotional and behavioural difficulties, repeat the process of Assess – Manage – Prevent.

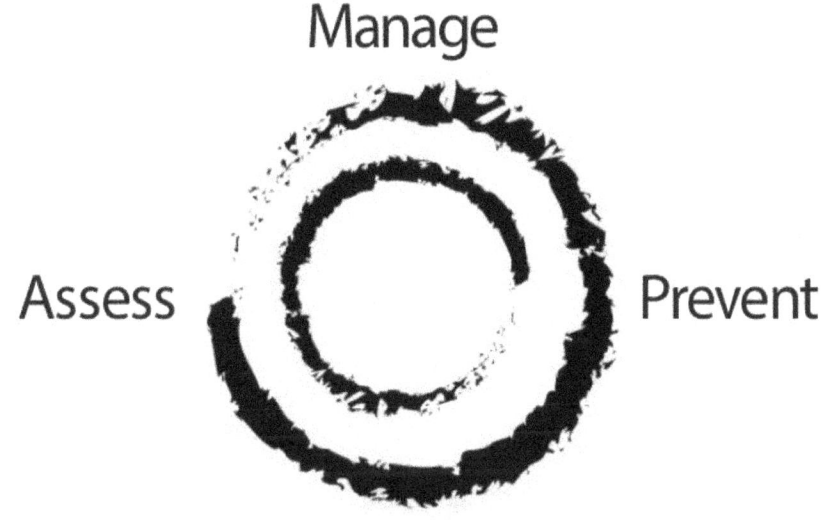

*When you plant lettuce, if it does not grow well, you don't blame the lettuce. You look into the reasons it is not doing well. It may need fertilizer, or more water, or less sun. You never blame the lettuce. Yet if we have problems with our friends or family, we blame the other person. But if we know how to take care of them, they will grow well, like lettuce. Blaming has no positive effect at all, nor does trying to persuade using reason and arguments. That is my experience. No blame, no reasoning, no argument, just understanding. If you understand, and you show that you understand, you can love, and the situation will change. Quote by Thich Nhat Hanh (1991)*

# REFERENCES

- American Psychiatric Association. (2013). <u>Diagnostic and Statistical Manual of Mental Disorders (5th Ed.)</u>. Arlington, VA: American Psychiatric Publishing.

- Carr, E. G., Levin, L., McConnachie, G., Carlson, J. I., Kemp, D. C. and Smith, C. E. (1994). <u>Communication-based intervention for problem behaviour: A user's guide for producing positive change</u>. Baltimore: Brookes.

- Griffiths, D. M., & Gardner, W. I. (2002). The integrated biopsychosocial approach to challenging behaviours. In D. M. Griffiths, C. Stavrakaki, and J. Summers (Eds.), <u>Dual diagnosis: An introduction to the mental health needs of persons with developmental disabilities (pp. 81–114)</u>. Sudbury, ON: Habilitative Mental Health Resource Network.

- Hanh, T. N. (1991). <u>Peace is every step: The path of mindfulness in everyday life</u>. New York: Bantam Books.

- Horner, R. H., and Diemer, S. M. (1992). <u>Educational support for students with severe problem behaviours in Oregon: A descriptive analysis from the 1987– 1988 school year. Journal of the Association for Persons with Severe Handicaps</u>, 17 (3), 154–169.

- Sugai, G. and Simonsen, B. (2012). <u>Positive Behaviour Interventions and Supports: History, Defining Features, and Misconceptions</u>. Retrieved 2018 January 8th http://pbis.org/school/pbis.revisited.aspx

# OTHER TITLES BY DOLLY BHARGAVA

## Emotional Regulation Series

Taking CHARGE of my Rainbow of Emotions

## Positive Behaviour Support Series

Positive Behaviour Support Strategies for Students with Attention Deficit Hyperactivity Disorder
Positive Behaviour Support Strategies for Students with Anxious Behaviour
Positive Behaviour Support Strategies for Students with Aggressive Behaviour
Positive Behaviour Support Strategies for Students with Autism Spectrum Disorder
Positive Behaviour Support Strategies for Students with Oppositional and Defiant Disorder

## A - Z of Challenging Behaviours Series

| | |
|---|---|
| A for Argumentative | H for Hyperactivity |
| A for Attention-Seeking | I for Impulsivity |
| B for Biting | K for Kicking |
| C for Cheating | L for Lying |
| D for Defiance | R for Repetitive Questioning |
| E for Excessive Reassurance Seeking | S for School Refusal Behaviour |
| E for Excessive Technology Use | S for Separation Anxiety |
| F for Flopping | S for Stealing |
| H for Hitting | T for Task Avoidance |

The list of titles is being expanded all the time. For the latest, please refer to www.behaviourhelp.com

**FOR MORE INFORMATION ON WORKSHOPS AND ONLINE TRAINING PLEASE VISIT WWW.BEHAVIOURHELP.COM**

www.ingramcontent.com/pod-product-compliance
Lightning Source LLC
Chambersburg PA
CBHW080226170426
43192CB00015B/2767